How Stories Really Work

Exploring the Physics of Fiction

by Grant P. Hudson B.A. (Hons.)

The Clarendon House Library

The Clarendon House Library consists of a range of materials covering the fields of fiction writing, essay writing, personal relationships, education, small business and more. What makes these materials unique is that they are based on an understanding of key fundamentals which underlie each of these fields which, if applied correctly, can transform each one into a successful enterprise.

All the materials are easy to read, informal in style and get swiftly to the point that the reader is most interested in. Many come with charts, diagrams and templates so that the reader can rapidly adapt what is learned and apply it quickly to, for example, a small business, a work of fiction, an essay or a personal relationship.

Clarendon House Publications is a small, independent publisher based online and in the UK. It is for anyone interested in writing (including fiction, essays, copywriting and anything to do with *Doctor Who*, comics, J. R. R. Tolkien, C. S. Lewis, literature and much more).

We hope that you will benefit from using these materials and look forward to receiving your feedback at

www.clarendonhousebooks.com

-The Editors

The programmes in this book have been included for their instructional value. They have been tested with care but are not guaranteed for any particular purpose. The publisher does not offer any warranties or representations nor does it accept any liabilities with respect to the programmes.

Published by Clarendon House Publications

ISBN #: 978-1-326-50726-8
Content ID: 18092599

Grant P. Hudson was born in Sheffield, South Yorkshire. In 1967, his family emigrated to Australia where he was educated. Returning to England in 1993, he worked as a management consultant, personal counsellor and many other things before teaching literature in a small independent school in Sussex in 1998, becoming the Head Teacher there before going into semi-retirement in 2014. He is the founder of Clarendon House Publications, an online venue for writers, self-publishers and others around the world.

He lives in Yorkshire with his wife and family.

WARNING:

The material in this book is dangerous.

It will almost certainly change the way you perceive any fiction you read or any film or play that you see.

Your appreciation of stories, your enjoyment of the movies, the thrill of the theatre, all these are about to change, to be enhanced, to be expanded upon. But be prepared: fiction - the art of constructing a tale from the imagination - is about to become transparent in ways you never thought possible.

Do not read this book unless you are prepared to deal with that.

This does not mean that you will never love a story again. This is about exploring, outlining and activating those forces that are already at work within stories and within readers which *you* can harness and control.

You are about to learn the true powers that are at the bottom of every adored protagonist, every hated antagonist, every plot that grips you, every message that impinges upon you. These powers are behind every successful piece of fiction, every satisfied reader. They are as potent as electricity, about as simple to understand and use - and about as dangerous.

Contents

A Brief Introduction

This book is a powerful tool for understanding fiction and for transforming your creative writing and taking it to new levels of clarity, energy and effectiveness.

In these pages, you will learn about:

• what a story *really* is and what it is actually doing to and for readers

• the *universal patterns* that all successful fiction follows to attract and grip readers

• the *magnetic power* that draws readers into a work of fiction *even before the introduction of any character*

• what the thing called a 'character' *actually* is, and the secrets of how to rapidly build a convincing one that attracts readers

• the things called 'plots', what they are and how they are actually made (rather than how you might suppose they are made)

• what a 'protagonist' *really* is and why this character is different to all the others

• what an 'antagonist' *really* is, and what the connection between him or her and the protagonist consists of

• the four categories of the *powerful force* that compels readers to turn pages

• the 'nuclear reactor' that drives all successful stories through to their conclusion

• how the four basic genres - Epic, Tragedy, Irony and Comedy - are composed and how they work to create different effects

• exercises that will help you to evaluate *exactly* where your fiction needs to change to be more successful

• the writing model which, if followed, will create a machine generating *unimaginable numbers of readers and heightened reader satisfaction* for you, based on some of the most successful pieces of literature in the English-speaking world.

Along the way, you'll discover:

• the presentational secrets that lie behind super-successful books and how you can use them in your fiction

• how to generate as much emotional commitment from readers as you want, stably and without any kind of 'trick'

• how to make sure you reach more readers by engaging with them in the proper way

• how you can add depth and meaning to any story so that your fiction resonates with readers and creates a desire to read it again and again

and much, much more.

Whether you want to be a better writer of fiction or simply understand how stories work, you've made a good choice. You'll find that this book doesn't waste a lot of your time - though there are some important theoretical things you'll need to grasp, there are no long chapters to bore or exasperate you. It's a steep learning curve at times, but we try to minimise using odd terminology that compels you to re-read page after page.

Though it's touched on, this book isn't about the 'Hero's Journey' - you can read about that elsewhere. The principles in this book explain *why* the Hero's Journey is such a common thing in fiction.

Nor does this book go into things like the 'three act structure' or where a climax occurs in a screenplay. There are plenty of works about all of that. *This book gives you the reasons why all those things work.*

This book is designed to be simple but effective. It's practical and pragmatic. It's based on hard experience from the teaching of literature; its theories have evolved from talking to students about the world's greatest authors for over twenty years. It's written to convey to you a tremendous amount in the shortest possible time. If by the time you reach the end you feel that you need further help in actually applying these ideas to your own writing, there's a companion volume - *How Stories Really Work -A Practical Manual to Transform Your Fiction* - full of templates, diagrams and exercises to guide you to do just that, and an e-course *How to Write Stories That Work - and Get Them Published!*, both available through the website:

www.clarendonhousebooks.com

This book calls upon a wide range of examples from the world of fiction - novels, adventure stories, plays, films, ancient and modern. Texts referred to or used as case studies in this book include Victorian novels, Shakepearian plays, children's stories, and modern novels, films, and television, including (but by no means limited to):

Tess Of The D'Urbervilles, by Thomas Hardy
A Passage to India, by E.M. Forster
The Lord of the Rings, by J.R.R. Tolkien
Dune, by Frank Herbert
Watership Down, by Richard Adams
Pride and Prejudice, by Jane Austen
To Kill a Mockingbird, by Harper Lee
Winnie the Pooh, by A.A. Milne
The Lion, the Witch and the Wardrobe, by C. S. Lewis
Jane Eyre, by Charlotte Brontë
Wuthering Heights, by Emily Brontë
The Wind in the Willows, by Kenneth Grahame
Great Expectations, by Charles Dickens
Harry Potter And The Philosopher's Stone, by J.K. Rowling
The Hobbit, by J.R.R. Tolkien
A Christmas Carol, by Charles Dickens
The Wizard of Oz, 1939
Groundhog Day, 1993
Emma, by Jane Austen
It's a Wonderful Life, 1946
Pulp Fiction, 1994
Star Wars, 1977
Back to the Future, 1985
Vertigo, 1958
Friends TV series 1994 - 2004
Captain America: The Winter Soldier, 2014
The Avengers, 2012

Every single one of these stories, and many more besides, use the principles described in this book, knowingly or not. As you will see, once you master these things for yourself, your own fiction could be transformed.

Spoiler Alert

It should be said that, in the course of discussing any story, vital facts about its characters and plot are often given away. It will be assumed that you will have read each story under discussion. If you don't want to find out something about a particular story, please skip the bit where it is being discussed!

Who am I?

I'm semi-retired. I've achieved most of what I wanted to do with my life and am concentrating on the last dream - being a writer.

I live where I want to live, with the people I want to live with, and spend most of my time doing the things I've always wanted to do.

But I am constantly asked for advice in a number of fields, especially in creative writing, education and business. Hence this book and a few others. The material here is all based on my own experience and knowledge. It is designed to help you to get into a similar position to the one I find myself in - without as much strife or as many mistakes on the way, it is to be hoped - in which stories literally fall apart in my hands, and from where you can see the 'code' which forms their fabric.

This book is not about instant gratification - though, if you apply its ideas, the probability is that your job satisfaction as a writer will markedly increase. This is all about getting it *right*, getting your act together and accomplishing your writing goals. If you want to look at fiction in an entirely new way, and use its principles to progress through a reasonable but not extraordinary amount of respectable work towards contentment, comfort and lasting, all-round satisfaction with your writing, read on.

How to Use This Book

This book uses various analogies with simple physics concepts - the kinds of things you learned in school. But don't worry - if you went blank in your science classes, it won't matter. It's basic stuff which is explained as you read along: things like gases, solids, liquids, vacuums and simple electronics. You won't have to know anything at all about science to follow it - and when you see the power of the analogies, your jaw will drop.

If you're serious about taking your fiction to the next level, this is for you. You'll have to implement each piece of advice, but the book will show you how to do that too.

Part One: Understanding Fiction covers the powerful, basic ideas that underlie everything to do with creative writing, readers, emotional commitment, presentation and so forth. At the end you will see what you have been doing and why it has either succeeded or failed so far, and you will have grasped the unique tools or weapons you need to take your writing to a whole new level.

Part Two: The Five Stage Fiction Model is a hands-on guide to implementation. Step by step you'll take everything you've learned and mould your work into a living machine which satisfies readers every time and which attracts emotion and positive word-of-mouth like a magnet.

At the end of the book is a Fiction Self-Assessment Questionnaire which will help to reveal where your creative writing is succeeding and failing right now. By then, you should have an idea of what you'll need to do to make it better.

What makes my approach different? I've worked in many different fields, education, business, recreation and others. In all of them, I have tried to discover the underlying basics which made each field work. And the basics of fiction are what this book is all about. Because there *are* basics; and when applied correctly they *do* work, unfailingly and with great power.

This isn't for the faint-hearted, the over-complicated, the too-cynical or the downright lazy. To achieve success using the principles in this book will take courage, simplicity, honesty and some hard work. But these things are to hand and the results are right around the corner. I look forward to hearing about your successes. Do this right, and there'll be plenty of those.

-Grant P. Hudson B.A. (Hons.)

Part One:

Understanding Fiction

Chapter One:
Making a Cup of Tea

You're a writer, or you want to be one.

You write, or want to write, something that someone else wants to read, wants to find fulfilling, and wants enough to pay you money for it.

Sounds simple, and it is - but there's an awful lot of complexity that can enter into that equation.

Chances are that you have run into at least one of the three most common barriers that any writer strikes:

1. You aren't actually writing.

This is the big one. You call yourself a writer, you really want to be a writer, your head is overflowing with ideas - but you aren't actually doing it. Your life is swallowed up by work, by children, by routines and relationships and remorseless demands which work against you actually sitting down and writing. This is the most common barrier: writers don't write.

2. You are writing, but you are not happy with the result.

Second biggest issue: you have commenced writing, perhaps you have even finished a first draft - but it's no good. You know it's not working. When you read it back to yourself - or, heaven forbid! to another - it sounds trite, boring, full of clichés. It wanders; it lacks drama; it doesn't end properly. Characters don't leap into life; the dialogue seems dull or unreal. In short, though you are proud of yourself for actually producing something, you know that it is a failure as a work of art.

3. You are writing, have produced something reasonable, but no one wants to publish it.

You're circulating a manuscript either among friends or among publishers, but get only rejection letters. Your friends are polite; even the publishers are polite - but no one is gagging to print and distribute your masterpiece to the hungry masses. It's just a dead weight, costing you postage.

In fact, you could probably place yourself somewhere on the following scale as a writer. (The last two columns have been left blank because the brutal truth is that it's unlikely you'd be reading this book if you were in those columns...):

Struggling...	Coping...	Feeling competent, but...	Published and happy...	Bestseller and writing a sequel...
You can't find time	You're putting something together bit and piece	You have a first draft but no one's interested		
You have ideas but forget what they are before you get a chance to note them down	You feel dispersed over so many notes	People are polite but not reaching for more		
Life swamps any attempt you make to write	You look back at what you've written and often tear it up or delete it	You know your work has problems but you're not sure what they are		
You feel completely apathetic	You daren't show your work to anyone	You have something that you feel passionate about and are frustrated that no one else feels the same		

The good news is that each one of these barriers has a remedy, and all the remedies are described in this book in such a way that you will be able to apply them with relative ease to yourself and your own work once you grasp them.

You can be a writer, and you can be successful; you can spot exactly what's wrong with your writing and fix it: your work can be moulded into shape and it can be made attractive to others, even publishers.

That's because there *is* a way of doing fiction properly - i.e. so that it *works*.

Where do you start?

Firstly, there's an incredibly simple idea which needs to be grasped so that these tools - and in fact your entire fiction - can be revitalised. It's to do with making a cup of tea. Bear with me - even if you don't like tea, these are the steps you first need to grasp if we are going to get anywhere.

Making a Cup of Tea

Making a cup of tea begins with the *idea* of making a cup of tea. You might be at work, or reading a magazine, or wandering about aimlessly - when you have the idea of making a cup of tea. You glimpse, with *foresight*, the satisfaction that it will bring.

Then there needs to be *someone to make it.* That might be you or another person. Some kind of organisation is needed, something has to be *formed*. It's not just going to appear out of thin air unless there's someone there. Either you have to do it yourself or attract someone else into doing it.

There needs to be a *desire* for a cup of tea to ensure that the idea actually begins to turn into reality. This is important. The idea of the cup of tea can and will stall right there unless the desire for it outweighs any kind of obstacle, unless your *familiarity* with having the cup of tea grows.

That desire results in a commitment. Certain materials are needed for the tea to be made: a kettle, a cup, the tea itself, milk and so forth - including Time. These have to be purchased. Your desire might be strong, but it has to be made strong enough for something to be *foregone* before any tea will be made.

Then the tea has to actually be made - in whatever sequence is right for you, milk in first or not. Boil the kettle, pour in the water and so forth, everything that is involved in *furnishing* an actual cup of tea. There are basics which can't be violated if you want something that remotely resembles a cup of tea.

The first sip tests the *quality* of the cup of tea. If it's not right, some adjustments will need to be made. How do you judge the quality? You match it against the earlier *desire*. If it is found wanting, the cup of tea has to be *fine-tuned* in some way to match that desire.

Then the cup of tea is finally *consumed*. You get the sense of *fulfilment* that you foresaw, perhaps, when you first had the idea.

It should be clear that if any one of these steps is not there, the whole product is not fully achieved.

Obviously, without the idea of making a cup of tea nothing even starts to happen.

If there's no one to make it, the idea won't get very far.

In the absence of any desire for a cup of tea, even if someone has the idea and there is someone to make it, there won't be sufficient motivation for anything to occur.

Without a kettle, a cup, the tea itself, milk and so on, there would be no cup of tea. If there's no real commitment or these can't be afforded, the idea dies right there.

If the notion gets as far as this, and the sequence of making it goes wrong, there goes the cup of tea.

If the quality of the cup of tea isn't good enough, it might as well not have been made.

And then, after all that, if the cup of tea sits untouched and unconsumed, the whole thing will have been a waste of time.

Each step, then, is essential.

What has this to do with your fiction writing?

Let's first of all explain a question of emphasis here. There are two aspects to this: yourself as a writer, and what you need to do to get up and running and writing the stuff you've longed to write; and the internal dynamics of your fiction, what makes the actual stories tick and what goes wrong with that mechanism which you can fix.

This book touches on both these aspects, but its primary emphasis is going to be on the second - what makes stories really work. If you can grasp that well enough, then the first aspect - how to become fully operational as a writer - will follow. But if you would like more advice on how to get to work as a writer, get the e-course *How to Write Stories That Work - and Get Them Published!*, which is available through the website www.clarendonhousebooks.com.

The First Thing You Have To Decide

The very first thing that you need to establish as a writer is this:

'What effect do you want to create for the reader?'

This can range from an obvious effect, like laughter, to a more subtle and mixed effect, like a feeling of enlightenment or elation about the world; it can be anything between an extreme of physical sensation to the other extreme of a purely intellectual idea.

Effects are normally grouped into two broad categories: positive, uplifting effects, and negative, introverting effects.

Another key question you should ask yourself is this:

'Why don't I just sum up the effect I want to create on readers in one sentence, or even in one word, and hand it to readers on a slip of paper straight away?'

In other words, why go to all the trouble of creating an effect on a reader through a *story*? If you want to make a reader laugh, why not just tell a joke right then and there? Why construct an elaborate world in which some kind of convincing comedy can take place? Why invent and insert these odd things called 'characters' and then manoeuvre them around into situations which readers will find amusing?

In other words, why try to create the effect through this thing called 'fiction'?

And what really is this thing called fiction anyway?

Here's a definition of fiction that will open the door to success and new worlds of creation:

Fiction is a set of procedures or tools used by writers to create specific effects upon readers.

Fiction writing is a kind of spell: you're trying, as a writer, to create an effect or set of effects on readers *without them knowing particularly what you are doing*. The effect has to somehow 'sneak up on them'. A fiction writer is really a master of illusion. Fiction is the difference between just telling a reader what effect you want to create and creating that effect beneath (or above) the reader's conscious awareness.

This book explores the secrets of that world of creating illusions, for the first time showing you how those illusions actually work.

Soon you will learn what the thing we have known as 'character' *really* is - as opposed to what you and many others might *think* it is.

Soon you will learn how a 'plot' *actually* works and what it is composed of - rather than what dozens of writing guide books tell you about it.

In the process of finding these things out, and discovering much more, you will begin to see the hidden 'code' behind any work of fiction and your purposes as a fiction writer will be invigorated in ways you couldn't have imagined.

In doing so, you will run into false ideas and perceptions that you have considered to be absolute truths in your career as a reader and a writer, things which are almost universally accepted but which can act as awful burdens unless you know the underlying truths that make them work.

For instance, you probably think of a character as 'a fictitious personality who, to be successful, must appear to be as lifelike as possible'.

You probably would swear by the datum that a plot, in order to attract readers, must contain something called 'conflict'. And you are probably very familiar with the idea that any work of fiction has to have 'at least three acts with a dramatic curve heading upwards to a climax, followed by a denouement'.

You've heard these things in schools, and elsewhere. You're surrounded by the vocabulary that comes with them. You've seen them at work in plays, films, novels.

By the time you get even partway through this book, you will see that all of these ideas are incomplete and can even be cumbersome in creating fiction that works.

Of course they all have workability. They are not nonsense. It's just that they all rest on deeper truths which are much simpler to apply.

Core Ideas

Successful fiction is made up of all the parts that we just covered in making a cup of tea and it has to do with the internal dynamics of stories as well as how you operate as a writer. The idea of making a cup of tea is like the ideas that underpin any piece of successful writing. It has to do with the heart of whatever it is you want to communicate as a writer, whether that's a very definite idea that you want others to understand, or an emotion that you want them to feel, or something intangible that you want them to experience.

Perhaps you've never thought of it quite like this before, but there will be something, or perhaps a series of things, that you *want to say* as a writer. You could write these things down as a list, but of course they would be simply soulless statements in list form. Nevertheless, those core ideas are the source of the whole enterprise of fiction writing - they are that part of the writing which underpins and creates the whole thing and plans and directs the work. Or they should be.

Within the story, these *core ideas* give rise to *themes*.

You don't see any simply-written, cold statement of the theme of psychosis in Shakespeare's *Macbeth* - nevertheless, psychosis as an idea stalks its pages in the language and comes to life in the play on the stage; you won't find a blunt anti-racist summary in Harper Lee's *To Kill a Mockingbird*, and yet every page communicates the novel's anti-racist message to the reader in various ways.

E. M. Forster's *A Passage to India*, for example, is superficially 'about' the conflicting cultures of the British and the Indians in the late nineteenth and early twentieth centuries. You could argue that the author's 'idea' is to do with that - but in fact the central idea of the novel, around which everything else is built, is much bigger and deeper than that. It has to do with the universe and meaning and beauty - it's very hard to sum up as a single blunt statement. Hence the need for a novel to communicate it. The novel itself is its *metaphor*; British and Indian relations are symbolic of something deeper and larger. You'll grasp the ramifications of this as we progress.

On a more popular level, it might be said that the *Star Wars* film series is about 'the Empire versus the Rebel Alliance, long, long ago in a galaxy far, far away' - and so it appears to be at first glance. But its success and resonance within popular culture suggest that the whole thing rests on more basic ideas, which we will explore later.

Characters

It's not enough to have an idea as a writer, even if it's a good one: you need to understand what the component parts of a successful text are, so that it actually *works* as a piece of fiction, not just a disguised essay about ideas.

One of these primary things is the item we currently know by the term 'character'. 'A character? That's just a person in a story - someone that things happen to, or who makes things happen, right?' Yes, but there's so much more to this that, once you have read the appropriate section in this book about character, *you will never see a single character in a story in the same way again!*

We warned you that this was dangerous!

Creating Desire

The desire for a cup of tea reflects the desire that there must in any piece of fiction if it is to succeed. It sounds too glib and simple, but readers have to really be engaged with a story for it to work in conveying your ideas. Increasing the desire of the reader produces the required level of commitment.

There have to be within the story fundamental *generators* which power the whole thing. No story, no matter how great the idea or even the structure, can survive longer than one page without these generators. What exactly they are and how they function is given in detail in later chapters.

When you take what you have known up until now as *character*, and then combine it with what you're about to find out about *generators*, you have in your hands explosive material.

Even having a slight grasp of these generators is a key step in bringing your fiction to life.

Emotional Commitment

What desire produces is *commitment*. Commitment leads to a willingness on the reader's part to *forgo* something. Readers in fact give writers permission to create effects on them. With some readers, this is easier than with others. Some readers resist having an effect of any kind created on them. It makes you wonder why they read at all - but they do, and if they do, you can get them to *commit*.

Just as certain materials are needed for tea to be made, any writer needs the certain key essentials in his or her work in order to be able to produce an effect upon a reader.

Every single successful story requires an exchange to take place between the reader and something in the fiction.

Emotion needs to be *paid out* by the reader; there needs to be some *forgoing*. Outwardly, this is the cash the reader pays to buy the book; inwardly, this is the emotional or spiritual commitment that the reader invests in the work because they see or feel a return on their investment. Without this capacity to obtain a deep commitment from the reader, a story will fail. Even if you've managed to hold the reader's attention until the end of the tale, the book will be cast aside and probably never read again.

If you want to write something which is *loved*, which is read *and re-read*, which actually has an *effect* on readers, which is then recommended to others, you need to be able to extract commitment from them.

Building a Plot

The tea has to actually be made and in any fiction writing the story has to be built, created, assembled, in a particular sequence. The writer has to actually put the time in and put the scenes onto a page or screen. This is the 'coalface', the interface between writer and reader, where things appear in the right order so that what the writer originally envisaged actually takes shape in the mind of the reader.

Within the tale itself, the plot has to move the reader forward and deliver an effect. Even in Jane Austen's *Emma*, for example, which students sometimes complain about as the novel in which 'nothing happens', there is a strand or sequence of motion or movement, commonly appearing as *events*, through which the reader moves towards the conclusion, where the final impact of the work is delivered.

Call this 'craft' or 'structure' or 'plot' - it's the series of choices, made by the writer, which actively and carefully shift the reader's attention around over a period of time.

All stories have Time in common, whether in prose or drama or even poetry: there is a movement, a progression from one thing to the next. But it is very much *their own time,* not necessarily - in fact, rarely - the time of the world around the book. This is the playing field where the writer furnishes what the reader wants, even if the reader doesn't know it yet.

There are specific plot mechanisms - four, in fact - that a successful writer uses to hold the reader gripped until the end of the story. You've never heard of them before in this way - but you have fallen under their spell every time you have read, heard or seen a story that has had an effect on you.

As a matter of fact, they're working on you right now, and this isn't even fiction.

Fine Tuning

As the quality of the cup of tea must be assessed, so must any writer have some way of judging the quality of what he or she is producing and delivering and ensuring that it matches the readers' needs. This sounds like common sense, but it becomes a little more opaque when you ask yourself 'By what criteria are we judging how close we are to a reader's needs?'

And 'What exactly *are* a reader's needs?'

Within the story itself, how does the aspect of quality manifest itself? What is happening on each page that tells us that we are getting nearer and nearer to (or further and further away from) the 'cup of tea' that was desired in the first place?

Just what exactly is your reader's 'cup of tea'?

Many aspects of this are fully explored in coming chapters. You'll learn how to use specific tools to ensure that your original effect actually arrives at the reader with full force.

Fulfilment

Where is all this heading? To the consumption of the 'cup of tea', the moment when the writer puts down his or her pen and the reader puts down the book. This is when the reader either has the feeling or receives the idea which marks the magical closure of the matter. This is the *Fulfilment* aspect. This is the aim of all fiction writing.

The *idea* has become form through the *character*; the *character* has attracted the reader; the reader has *committed* to the book. This has led to the *furnishing* of the story, *fine tuned* to meet exact needs. That leads to *fulfilment*, the Holy Grail of all fiction writing.

You will soon see which part of this is working well in your fiction, and which part isn't working well or is perhaps missing entirely. Firstly by knowing what is and isn't present, and then by seeing what needs to be done to have all of these aspects working for you, you can transform your fiction in ways you never dreamed were possible.

The Spectrum of Fiction

We're going to assume a couple of things here:

1. That you have some kind of work of fiction either written or in your head and

2. That it involves something that you want a reader to experience.

Fiction, at its best, is a way of conveying something to a reader.

Perhaps you've never thought of it like that before. Most would-be writers haven't - indeed, many actual writers haven't. But it's true to say that the best fiction out there has one thing in common: *it successfully conveyed something to a reader*. That 'something' might have been joy, elation or a sense of victory; it might have been sadness, pity or a feeling of loss. Perhaps it was a sense of desperation or despair; perhaps it was laughter, relief or contentment. Or maybe it was a combination of many of these things and others, subtle or unsubtle.

Undeniably, though, all successful fiction conveys *something*. The least successful fiction is merely the ramblings of the author, and fails to connect to any reader or to bring about any transfer of knowledge, emotion or thought; the most successful fiction feels as though it is taking place in our own minds rather than that of an author whom we have never met; it connects with us on levels we didn't know we had; and from it we gain insight, awareness and ideas that are hard to describe in any way other than through the story itself.

To put it another way:

A successful piece of fiction exactly matches needs in a reader, even if the reader wasn't aware of the needs in the first place.

It has to match the needs before it can be called a success.

That might include a need for a whole range of vicarious experiences; it might be a need for communion with our fellow human beings, for emotions, for insights, for wonder, for sensations, for escapism or for confrontation or anything in-between. When the need is matched, the fiction is successful. What's the difference between success and failure in fiction?

Successful fiction is written for readers; unsuccessful fiction is written for writers.

Take a look at this scale. Any work of fiction lies somewhere along this scale, which we can call the Spectrum of Fiction:

THE SPECTRUM OF FICTION

WRITER-ORIENTATED

Reader struggles to have empathy with text

Reader feels excluded and alienated by text

Reader rejects and dismisses text

Reader only occasionally experiences text internally, but inconsistently

Reader only occasionally feels direct, subjective ideas and emotions from text

Reader experiences partial, perhaps temporary shift in viewpoint

READER-ORIENTATED

Reader experiences text as though in his/her own head

Reader gains direct, subjective ideas and emotions from text

Reader is endowed with gains or a shift of viewpoint from the text

The name of the game of this book is to move your fiction to the right along this spectrum, so that each and every piece of fiction you construct is achieving powerful effects upon readers.

How can this be done? Partly by encouraging you to 'unlearn what you have learned', as Master Yoda says in *The Empire Strikes Back*.

Fiction is a fantastic, wonderful and magical machine which can take you just about anywhere and have you experience just about anything - but it's a machine, nonetheless.

Like a machine, it has component parts, and like a machine, it only works if those components are all present and are assembled in the right sequence. Like a machine, fiction only works if it has the right fuel. Like a machine, fiction can break down unless all of these things are kept smoothly running by the writer.

Are we talking about things like words and grammar? They are a small part of this, less than 1%. We are talking about the principles that lie *behind* the 'hero's journey' or the three act structure or climaxes and so forth. We are talking about concepts which, once you properly appreciate them, will change the way you look at stories forever. These things are not mystical; we're talking about understanding the things that lie behind great works of fiction all over the world.

Writer-centric or Reader-centric?

Though all creative works are very different in character and nature, *they all follow patterns which can be understood and managed.* That's because they are all based on *need.*

Fulfilment of some kind of need is the end product of every successful piece of fiction.

If your writing is struggling in any way, the engine that is Need needs an overhaul.

By a 'successful piece of fiction' is meant *one which has a consistent, high-volume flow of readers who then leave very happy with what you have done for them, spreading positive word-of-mouth which brings in more and more new readers.*

As we have touched on, any and all fiction, to be proper fiction at all, must or should be concerned with one thing and one thing only:

The end product of any work of fiction is to bring together the reader and the thing that the reader needs or wants in an exact match.

Many writers, in ignorance of this, tend to believe that readers are going to be somehow interested in what the writer has to offer regardless of their needs. They build a 'writer-centric' model. And then grow more and more frantic as it fails. 'Fiction' that is writer-centric appears to be mainly just creative writing put together by people in the hope that someone will read it. But you can't just create pieces of writing in whatever way you like and expect them to be read. If you don't get a reader's interest, you don't get a sale and you don't get a lasting success - and therefore certainly not reader commitment. Whether you want your reader to be excited by your fast-paced political thriller or to walk away with a changed view about a social theme or to contemplate an experience with a warm glow of satisfaction, you need to ensure that *your reader follows you all the way*, that you 'get' what he or she wants, and that you provide *exactly that*. Otherwise you'll end up very much to the left of the Spectrum of Fiction above.

This book is about being able to build a properly effective 'reader-centric' piece of fiction.

Does this mean that you have to write for others only? That you are somehow prevented from writing for your own satisfaction?

Quite the opposite.

What it means is that you will understand, perhaps for the first time, what it is that readers need - *including yourself as a reader*. Your fiction will be immediately transformed into a more effective, more powerful and more interesting piece of work *for you as well as for other potential readers*.

The Purpose of Your Fiction

What is your writing there to do? Is it there to make you money? To manufacture works that you then have to work extremely hard to sell? To scour the world for readers while you still have some strength left?

Flip it around. Look at it from the viewpoint of a potential reader.

Your fiction exists to fill a vacancy for a reader.

If you have that vacancy correctly defined, the reader will simply flow towards your work. In the absence of a definition of the vacancy, you may abandon the effort altogether. Your reader almost certainly will.

Your potential readers are motivated by forces which largely remain invisible to you.

What would happen to your fiction if you could 'read the minds' of every single one of the people approaching your books? What do you think would occur if you could base the details or presentation of your stories on the real motivations and impulses underlying your readers' needs?

Two things would happen:

• reader satisfaction would sky-rocket, leading to escalating loyalty and return sales

and

• positive word-of-mouth would ripple outwards from each reader, resulting in more and more readers.

The truth is that it is possible to develop an ability to see into the worlds of your potential readers. This power is not supernatural or psychic but very real. Using it, you can tap into the forces which drive every single reader and completely transform your fiction.

Every single successful piece of fiction, whether a novel, a play, a short story or a film, uses this power.

What is this 'hidden force'?

Chapter Two:
Vacuum Power

What motivates people? Goals? Targets? Money?

No.

Nothing.

Literally, 'nothing'.

By 'nothing' is meant a *gap,* something *missing,* an *emptiness.* This could also be termed a *mystery,* an *absence,* a *loss,* a *lack,* a *want,* an *unavailability,* a *deficiency,* an *omission,* an *exclusion,* or a *need.*

Yes, of course we can set goals and of course they have to be desirable. But what is it that actually starts someone moving, physically or mentally, towards that goal?

The vacuum between where they are now and the goal.

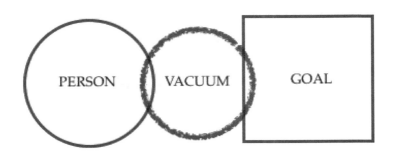

That's what pulls people forward.

You need a goal, a mountain top, something to aim for, certainly. But that target, whatever it is, *is defined by its absence.* Right now, you don't have it; right now, there's nothing there; right now, there's a *vacuum.*

It can be simply stated - so simply, that at first your mind may reject it.

Set a goal - any goal - and you immediately activate the pulling power of its absence.

Why is this such a secret?

Because an emptiness, a nothing, is almost by definition, *invisible.* When we think of something we want to achieve, we picture it perhaps, or write it down, or discuss it with someone. But none of those things have much power to move us, despite what all the books on visualisation say.

What moves us is the vacuum power of the goal or target that is not yet there.

Just as a vehicle is sucked into the slipstream of a juggernaut on the motorway, or a boiled egg is sucked into the emptiness of a heated bottle, or an astronaut is sucked out into the vacuum of space through a broken hatch, so we are moved by the power of emptiness.

Desire creates emptiness. Emptiness moves us.

You have a goal. You can write it down, picture it, mock it up in a stage and hang it on your wall. You can do any number of things with it. But what pulls you into actually moving towards that goal is *the emptiness between you and it.*

Everyone has these emptinesses. They are needs. We have small needs like the need for a snack or a cup of tea; we have larger needs like the need for a rest or companionship; and we have huge needs like the need for water, health and life itself. The best term to describe them is 'vacuums' because we are all familiar with the basic idea of the power of vacuums in one way or another either from school or because we've used a vacuum cleaner.

A vacuum, if it's strong enough, can make anyone do anything.

This is such a simple idea that it is easy to dismiss. But simplicity is power.

Understand this one and the world is yours to command.

This should change your ideas of what a writing goal is. Or even what a goal is generally.

What are some usual goals?

Wealth?

Property?

Love?

Happiness?

What lies between a person and these goals?

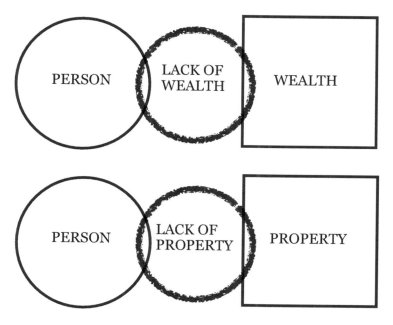

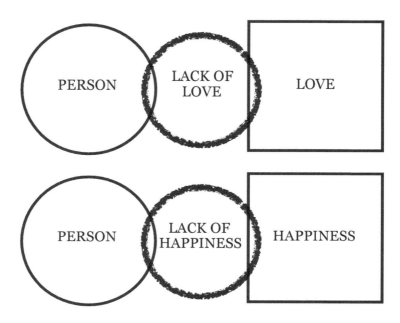

The bigger or more intense the vacuum, or lack, or absence, the more powerful the pull.

Setting a Goal

The usual advice that you can read in a thousand other books about achieving goals is to set the goal and then break that goal down into achievable targets and plan how to achieve those. That's all very well and can work - *but what drives this is the emptiness between the starting point and the goal.*

Actually sometimes breaking the goal down into smaller, do-able parts works to *reduce* its vacuum power. Larger goals and challenges can often possess more vacuum power.

To put it even more simply will reduce it to an almost absurd tautology. But here goes:

If I want a new kitchen table and a new kitchen table exactly like the one I want suddenly appears in front of me, what happens to my want? It vanishes. I have no need to go to the furniture shop. I have no need to move at all.

If I want a new kitchen table, what is it that makes me get up and go and get one? The *absence* of that table, the fact that it is *missing*, the *vacuum* created by its absence.

It would be as though there is a vacuum, shaped exactly like the table I want, sitting in the middle of the room. What will it take to fill it? Something will have to happen; things will have to occur in the universe; action will have to take place. Is this action caused by the table? No, quite the reverse. If the table appears, there is no need for action. The action is caused by the *absence of the table*.

People motivated to achieve wealth are motivated by the absence of wealth.

People motivated to acquire property are motivated by the absence of property.

People motivated by achieve love are motivated by the absence of love.

People motivated by a desire for happiness are motivated by the desire more than the happiness.

It's such a simple principle, but the world of fiction writing will open up to its full richness if you can apply this principle completely.

Why isn't this more widely known?

It sort of is. It's the principle behind every successful novel, every movie deal, every closed sale, every satisfied reader or viewer.

People are motivated by emptinesses, lacks, missing things, absences.

For the purposes of this book, we are going to call these things *vacuums* because what we know about vacuums in the physical universe will help us to understand how they work.

Here's some text book definitions of a 'vacuum':

vacuum: *'A space entirely devoid of matter; a space or container from which the air has been completely or partly removed; a gap left by the loss, death, or departure of someone or something formerly playing a significant part in a situation or activity.'*

Of course, as we know 'Nature abhors a vacuum' and vacuums tend to suck things into them or to have an attractive power with regard to their surroundings.

We can slightly re-define this for our purposes based on what we know about the properties of vacuums.

A vacuum is defined as that emptiness or absence of something which draws anyone or anything in the vicinity of the vacuum towards whatever it is that is missing.

Thus a need, a desire, a yearning, a longing, has the power to draw the person who has it towards the object of that need, desire, yearning or longing.

This is the primary force which underlies how human transactions work, including transactions between a reader and a piece of fiction.

If you need further convincing, let's step back for a moment and look at what happens in fiction today.

Vacuum Power in Fiction

The word fiction is usually defined along these lines:

fiction: literature in the form of prose, especially novels, that describes imaginary events and people.

It comes from late Middle English (in the sense 'invented statement') via Old French from Latin *fictio*(n-), from *fingere* 'form, contrive'. The whole idea behind the idea is that it is to do with *things that are made up*.

And so it starts from a 'writer-centric' perspective: whatever a writer wants, thinks or feels should happen next is 'right'. And so fiction writers sit at their desks or in the chairs and write whatever they imagine. And that's fiction.

The biggest problem with all that is that *there is absolutely no guarantee that anything that emerges from a writer's mind will be of any interest whatsoever to a reader.*

90% of writers, whether they are young or old, new or have been attempting to write a book for years, experience this:

They write and write and write and then don't know where the thing is going and end up running out of steam and abandoning the story.

Page after page, chapter after chapter, draft after draft, manuscript after manuscript. This is why writers give up. Or, if they persist, why they are still failures even years down the line.

After all, the aim of every writer should be to just write, right? Commitment from readers will eventually come, right? It's all a numbers game and, with a bit of luck and a fortunate encounter with a positive publisher, success will come, right?

Wrong.

Writing for its own sake as an aim of fiction is based on a completely inaccurate understanding of what successful fiction is. If you think that simply by putting words on a page or screen straight from your head you will eventually end up 'striking it rich' in terms of reader commitment, then by all means continue to pour out your imagination onto the page or screen. Less than 1% of successful writers succeed that way *and they eventually succeed because they hit by accident upon some of the principles described in this book.*

Reader Commitment

If you more correctly see that reader commitment is something that is generated and passed on as the result of *something else*, then suddenly you can appreciate that just generating volume writing for its own sake produces a lot of wasted paper. Writing page after page without consulting the needs of readers produces in the writer a deep sense of alienation, self-deception and a mounting feeling that the universe is unfair and doesn't recognise genius.

Do you recognise those thoughts and feelings?

Let's not be misunderstood here: there's nothing wrong with writing straight from your head or with producing lots of it. But if you set 'just writing' as the uppermost goal of a writing life, *it will ultimately lead to the downfall of yourself as a writer.*

What should the uppermost goal of a fiction writer be, then?

Everyone has goals, and everyone, therefore, is surrounded by emptinesses which precede or cluster around these goals: needs, or as we are going to call them, *vacuums*. These vacuums draw a person towards anything which looks as though it might fill the vacuum. Thus a person might need a new watch or be desperately searching for a cure for migraines or be looking to order a pizza for a large family, or be seeking a lost friend or fleeing a war in search of sanctuary. Each of these things is a vacuum of a particular kind. There are lots of kinds and sizes of vacuums, as you will learn, but for now it's the basic principle that we have to take in.

Everyone has vacuums.

If everyone is walking around driven by their needs, what are they looking for? Something that will *fulfil* their needs. What should your fiction be in that case?

Works of fiction are vacuum-fillers.

If your writing is built around that datum, all shall be well.

But the idea of vacuum power opens the world up to new possibilities. The first thing to do, obviously, is to establish what exactly your readers needs are and then work to fulfil them. But how do you generate interest and energy and movement and forward progress?

How do you attract hordes of readers and guarantee that they will be happy?

You can see that setting goals is one thing - harnessing the vacuum power around those goals is something else. To be truly and spectacularly effective, goals should harness the maximum number and size of vacuums of everyone involved. And if you look at any goal that anyone has ever achieved, it's usually by tapping into the goals and vacuum power of those around them too.

A writer who has these all aligned and active would harness enough power to take over the world. A writer who even bothers to ask what the vacuums of his or her readers are, let alone activates or aligns them, will ignite attractive power and become effective.

Fiction is an operation of ideas built around vacuums.

That looks like a re-definition of fiction itself.

The Power of Fiction

What exactly is a 'vacuum filler' in a work of fiction?

Consider the most powerful, memorable moments in your own reading. Think for a moment about the scenes in your favourite books or films which created 'goosebump' sensations for you. Try to recall the exact incidents which had the most lasting effect on you as a reader.

Here are some examples:

• the sense of imparted wisdom and humanity at the end of Harper Lee's *To Kill a Mockingbird*

• the awestruck silence at the end of Shakespeare's *Hamlet*

• the feeling of emotional and social satisfaction at the end of Austen's *Pride and Prejudice*

• the chilling moment of unsolved mystery at the end of J. B. Priestley's *An Inspector Calls*

• the uplifting emotion of triumph at the end of Richard Donner's *Superman* film

• the glimpse of transcendent worlds at the ends of C. S. Lewis's novels *Perelandra* or *The Last Battle*.

Of course, vacuum fillers produced by fiction are too numerous to list. That's because they exist in microcosm by the thousand in any successful work of fiction, and also come at the end of every successful story that there has ever been, to one degree or another.

These moments, these experiences, have something in common. For the majority of stories, they concern a gap being repaired, an emptiness being filled, a hope fulfilled, something missing being found.

J. R. R. Tolkien coined a word for this in his 1947 essay 'On Fairy Stories': *eucatastrophe*. Eucatastrophe means the sudden turn of events at the end of a story which ensures that the protagonist does not meet some terrible, impending doom which has been growing more and more imminent as the story goes on. Tolkien formed the word by affixing the Greek prefix *eu*, meaning *good*, to *catastrophe*, the word traditionally used to refer to the 'unraveling' or conclusion of a drama's plot. It describes that uplifting and unexpected moment when 'everything goes right' beyond anyone's hopes.

As a devout Roman Catholic, Tolkien calls the Incarnation of Christ the eucatastrophe of 'human history'.

Here are some examples of eucatastrophe:

• the destruction of the Death Star towards the end of *Star Wars: A New Hope*

• the final critical scene atop Mount Doom in *The Lord of the Rings*

• the closing scene of Frank Capra's classic film *It's a Wonderful Life*.

You will probably have thought of several more. Though events were plummeting towards death or at least devastation, something occurs which not only restores order but which suggests the operations of a benevolent Providence over the world of the story.

These kinds of moments occur in so many stories: *Watership Down*, by Richard Adams, *Pride and Prejudice*, by Jane Austen, *Jane Eyre*, by Charlotte Brontë, *The Wind in the Willows*, by Kenneth Grahame, *Anne Of Green Gables*, by L. M. Montgomery, *A Christmas Carol*, by Charles Dickens, *The Wizard of Oz*, 1939, *Groundhog Day*, 1993, *Back to the Future*, 1985, and so on.

Not all stories contain them, though. *Tess Of The D'Urbervilles*, by Thomas Hardy, *A Passage to India*, by E. M. Forster, *Wuthering Heights*, by Emily Brontë, *Great Expectations*, by Charles Dickens, *Animal Farm* and *1984* by George Orwell are examples where far from everything going right the reader experiences, and is sometimes left in, at least one nightmare moment where everything has in fact gone terribly wrong. What is happening in these stories?

As we will see, stories which end in joy or triumph and those which end in sorrow or nightmare are all part of a universe of stories which all use vacuum power. Sometimes the vacuums are left empty. Instead of eucatastrophe, there's just catastrophe.

The truth is that the power of any work of fiction, whether it ends in positivity or not, depends upon these moments of fulfilment. They are usually to do with the filling of a vacuum of some kind, or, if the story is to have a negative ending, the emptiness which comes from *not* filling a vacuum.

When the gaping emptiness which is craving fulfilment is *not* filled and left open and hollow, that also has a resonant effect - but it is still dependent in the first place on there being a huge gap that needs to be filled.

Prior to that climactic moment of fulfilment, the reader was drawn in and made some kind of emotional commitment to the story, otherwise the fulfilment scene would be hollow and would fail. At some point in all the stories we have used as examples, readers made an investment of time and feeling: the destruction of the Death Star would be just another special effect unless somehow our emotions had been elicited; the final scene on Mount Doom would be an empty volcanic explosion in *The Lord of the Rings* had we not committed ourselves to feel something earlier in the tale; the finale of *It's a Wonderful Life* would not much concern us, having to do with the life of a small town businessman, as it does, had we not been drawn in to identify with George Bailey on deeper levels.

Similarly, Tess's end in *Tess Of The D'Urbervilles* could hardly have any effect had we not begun to profoundly wish that her life had turned out otherwise. *A Passage to India*, *Wuthering Heights*, *Great Expectations*, and so on all leave us with heartfelt revelations of some kind, hard to reduce to words, but scarcely less powerful than the triumphant endings in earlier examples.

These works are all doing the same thing.

Effective works of fiction construct vacuums for the reader, whether or not the vacuum is filled at the end.

This has very little to do with the common image of writers pouring their souls onto the page and somehow, some kind of arcane magic then affecting readers to like their work. It has a great deal to do with engineering into place a variety of specific vacuums which all act to draw in reader commitment and set up the reader for the positive or negative legacy of the end of the tale.

A person's attention will *automatically* be pulled towards a vacuum in the same way that water is pulled down a drain, or that a stone, thrown up in the air, is pulled down again by gravity. Vacuums exert a mental force equivalent to a physical force in the outer world.

But these things are not just randomly generated. There are specific kinds of vacuums in every work of fiction: specifically, five types, used in different ways and to varying degrees to create almost every story you can think of.

Let's start by examining the first type.

Chapter Three:
Character Vacuums

The classic definition of a character is along the lines of 'a created being who has needs, just like a person, with a background or biography full of fascinating details', all designed to make the constructed person more interesting to the reader.

Though something like this has been used both to describe characters in fiction and to offer advice to creative writers for as long as there have been stories, it is actually misleading.

The entity which we have been accustomed to calling a 'character' is actually *a construction of vacuums.*

If you design one of these 'characters' to have a well-rounded life, being content in a job, living comfortably with an ideal family life, your construct will not generate much energy in any story.

Any entity that we call a 'character' only becomes interesting *when something is taken away from him or her.*

If a constructed character has a damaged life, is unhappy in a job, lives uncomfortably and has a far from ideal family life, he or she will generate energy in your story. The character - and more importantly, the reader - will have attention on his or her vacuums and will be pulled by them into the story, either in the short or long term.

Stories are conventionally divided into two broad types: 'plot-driven' or 'character-driven'.

Both plot-driven and character-driven stories are vacuum-driven.

It's simply a matter of placing the vacuums correctly. How do you successfully construct characters and motivate them?

The thing to keep in mind is this:

Motivation is always vacuum-driven.

Character Motivation

What we are used to calling 'motivation' is the phenomenon arising from *something being missing*. The missing item, mood or state is what pulls people - including artificially-constructed people - into doing anything. If people seem to lack motivation, they lack vacuums; if they are super-motivated, they have powerful vacuums. In fiction, these vacuums can largely be determined by you or not as a writer.

Does this mean *removing* family, health, salary, comfort, job satisfaction and much more from the happy character in order to create an 'absence' which will then create motivation?

Yes!

Does it mean trying to solve the discontentment of the unhappy character? No! Not at first anyway, and sometimes not at all.

'Characters' come alive and lead readers forward through a rhythm of vacuums and vacuum fillers - they lose, they find; they don't have, they have; they lack, they get.

But mainly they *lose*.

Before he gets anywhere near the Death Star in *Star Wars: A New Hope,* Luke has lost almost everything: his old lifestyle, his real parents, his foster parents, and his newly found mentor. The removal of each one created a vacuum which pulled him into further action as a character. Prior to returning home after visiting Ben Kenobi, Luke had no plans to follow the old man or learn the ways of the Force, even though his missing father had done so. Only when he sees his home in flames and the charred remains of his foster parents does he make that forward-moving decision.

Frodo in *The Lord of the Rings* has also given up everything - or had it taken from him: the Shire, his friends, his health, his freedom, and at the end even one of his fingers. The heavy burden of loss and threat of loss is what moves him forward. Whenever motivation seems lacking, he suffers another loss: he loses consciousness and physical well-being after the stabbing on Weathertop, he loses Gandalf after the journey through Moria, he loses the rest of the Fellowship after Boromir's betrayal, and so on. Each removal serves to magnify the vacuum power and move him on as a constructed character (and move us on as readers).

George Bailey in *It's a Wonderful Life* has a persisting ambition to leave his small home town and make something of himself. This is progressively taken away from him until he is a shell of a man towards the end of the film - but then, after he himself is 'edited' out of his own life and becomes a ghost or walking vacuum, the vacuum is filled with powerful eucatastrophic effect at the end of the film.

Character constructs like Tess in *Tess Of The D'Urbervilles*, Adela Quested in *A Passage to India*, Cathy in a *Wuthering Heights*, or Miss Havisham in *Great Expectations*, are similarly 'walking vacuums', their lives emptied and hollowed out by events. In their cases, the emptiness is *not* filled, leaving a distinctly different flavour to the stories in which they feature.

In all stories, though, the things which we have been accustomed to call 'characters' are really *constructs* - and the primary building material for each is *vacuums*.

Creating successful fictional characters means *creating or finding vacuums which will pull in reader attention.*

In the same way that a reader is pulled along by vacuums of his or her own creation or those created by others in life, so is a character almost physically pulled into action on a scene-by-scene basis. The vacuums are either

• his or her own, directing energies and attention onto personal concerns or things that he or she wants or needs to have in the context of the story ('character-driven')

or

• are created by others and then impinge upon the character ('plot-driven').

If you want more productive work from either a happy character or an unhappy character, *find and create vacuums.*

The reason that a journey or quest motif is so common in fiction, especially fiction for younger readers, is that a journey or a quest is based on a simple *vacuum:* the hero needs to get somewhere where he or she isn't at the beginning; or to find something which he or she doesn't have at the beginning. The 'quest' belongs to a particular category of plot vacuum that we will get to shortly.

The gap between the existing state of affairs and achieving the target is the vacuum that pulls the character along.

Obviously, you need to set such targets realistically. Use judgement and establish agreement with the character and you will find forward motion occurring. This is the force which draws your protagonist out of his or her initial environment and into the new worlds that the rest of the story has in store.

The key advice is:

If you want character motivation, create vacuums.

Character Vacuums and Plot

Your characters have to have vacuums - missing things, losses, damage, needs - which then attract reader attention. And then your plot has to have vacuums - missing things, losses, spaces - which move things forward. We will examine the four main types of plot vacuum shortly.

The closer you can get the character vacuums to coincide with the plot vacuums, the better your story will be.

For example, in *Great Expectations*, Pip thinks that if he journeys to London and learns to become a gentleman, he will win Estella whom he loves but who torments him.

Or, from *The Lord of the Rings*, if Frodo journeys to Mordor with the Ring, he will save the Shire and everyone in it from the devastation that Sauron will bring.

Or, from *Pride and Prejudice*, if Lizzy Bennett can find a husband, she can rescue her family from imminent ruin.

Sometimes a story is completely plot-driven. *Indiana Jones and the Raiders of the Lost Ark*, for example, is a series of events which are naturally pulled forward by vacuums which don't have much to do with individual characters. It's been said that Indiana Jones could be entirely missing from the film and the events would still occur much as they do anyway. In this case, his character vacuums - his hunger for artefacts as an archaeologist, mainly - run *alongside* the events of the story.

In *Wuthering Heights*, on the other hand, the plot springs largely from the vacuums of the characters: it is Heathcliff's and Cathy's passion for each other which drive the events and almost all other relationships in the story.

Either way, the driving force is *something missing* - a vacuum or set of vacuums. If the vacuum is made real enough, and is strong enough, the character will swing round and align his or her actions with the plot and you will have a believable, powerful story.

If a character possesses no vacuums, it's probably time to let that character go before any more damage is done to your story, or inject vacuums into him or her. The vacuum-less character simply doesn't align and can't be aligned with whatever it is that you want to write about. He or she is 'dead'.

Writers often think that a character they have devised is 'not working' and so try to *add* qualities, characteristics or even accessories in the hope of generating interest. The opposite is true: *remove* qualities, characteristics and accessories and they will leap into life.

Character motivation is defined as the art of locating the vacuum which has sufficient pulling power to produce needed action.

Dealing with characters, therefore, is much the same as dealing with readers: it's all about *creating or finding vacuums and filling them.*

Growing Vacuums

Character constructs develop along particular lines. At first, a character may have no awareness of anything missing in his or her life; then there may be a vague awareness, followed by a larger or growing need, leading to a desperate desire.

Take a look at this diagram:

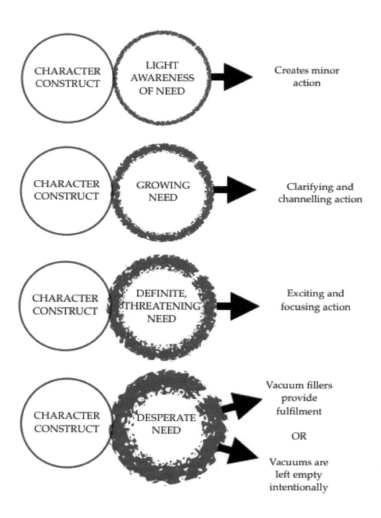

For those characters who have little or no idea of their need, your story has to *create* it. This depends on what elements you choose to remove from the construct and how you present them. You'll get specific advice on how to start with this soon.

For those who have only a vague notion of their need, your story has to *clarify and channel it*. What are the key factors which grab that construct's attention? These are the things which move your character into action.

Once your character has a larger need, your next step is to *excite and focus* it. This includes all the technology you're about to learn about character and plot vacuums and so forth which is designed to guide things forward, compelling your reader to turn each page until the end.

The stage of desperate need occurs when you have obtained the emotional commitment from the reader and you simply have to *point the reader in the right direction and remove barriers between the reader and the vacuum filler*. This has to do with, and defines, the 'climax' of the story. This is when the vacuum filler, the moment of fulfilment, takes place.

A work of fiction that does all or most of these things will attract readers through these character constructs and drive them through right to the end of the story.

Harry Potter had no inkling that he was a wizard at the beginning of his adventures. He just knew somehow that something was fundamentally wrong in his life. J. K. Rowling had taken away his freedom and happiness, creating an initial character vacuum. Once he discovers something about his true heritage, and realises what was missing, he is motivated and becomes active. The rest of the Harry Potter stories are chiefly powered by the four kinds of plot vacuum, as we will see.

If this is the case, then, why do so many works fail? What is going on in the fiction world that these apparently simple principles don't get applied and readers are soon lost even if they are initially acquired? If everything above is known and obvious, then surely it's too easy and anyone could be a successful fiction writer?

Something seems to go wrong right at the heart of many attempted works which causes the above simplicities to be obscured and everything to become so much more hard work and struggle than it needs to be. The answer is that, apart from not knowing about vacuums and how to build them, writers also often fail to build *enough* vacuums.

Vacuum building doesn't end with engaging the reader.

Surely engaging the reader is the entire point and purpose of vacuums? Yes, obtaining engagement from readers is a major part of what you are trying to do - but it's not the whole picture. Vacuum building *doesn't* actually end with getting a reader: you can actually go on and on using the vacuum generation approach described in this book to get *commitment* after *commitment* after *commitment* - which is the key to escalating reader engagement - as long as you focus on *getting a finely-tuned vacuum filler, otherwise known as a moment of fulfilment, into the heart of your reader.*

In other words, if a work's whole attention is on obtaining the reader's engagement as a final product, then the work will end up eventually losing readers in the longer term. You have to become an experienced practitioner at creating vacuums and then filling them - and then creating even more vacuums.

Together, vacuum building and getting readers are, once you grasp these principles, becoming a science, like physics. And if you learn that science and apply it, you'll get dependable results every time with your fiction. But like any science that is trying to be a technology, it has to *do* something.

Different Kinds of Vacuums

Please remember that whenever we use the word 'vacuum' we are talking about *need*. The point of using the word 'vacuum' and not 'need' - and calling it *vacuum power* rather than 'need power' - is that the word 'vacuum' suggests qualities and characteristics which are more helpful in understanding what is happening with readers than the word 'need' does.

What do we know about vacuums from basic science? As we have seen, a vacuum is defined as a space or container from which the air has been completely or partly removed. What happens in the vicinity of vacuums? Surrounding air or objects are pulled toward a vacuum until it is filled. The bigger the vacuum, the stronger the pull. Vacuums create attraction. They have a *pull*.

Readers of various kinds are walking around the world, carrying with them their own inner needs. They may not be aware of these vacuums; they may only have some slight inkling of them; they may be urgently aware of them and trying to deal with them; or they may feel that the vacuums are not pressing.

That's what makes a reader a reader: a reader is someone with an *actual* or *potential* vacuum.

That means just about anyone who is alive, right?

Right.

So the job of a successful fiction writer is to find or create character vacuums that resonate with reader vacuums.

The 'vacuum' could be a need or casual desire for escape, a need to feel an emotion, a desire for a deeper understanding; it could be vicarious sensation, a sense of relief, a get-away from mundanity, a new look at things, or even peace of mind. The range of effects that could be described in terms of vacuums is infinite. As there are many different kinds and categories of vacuums, a special glossary has been put together at the end of this book. But for now it will help to examine specific types of *character vacuums*.

There are four basic kinds of character vacuum:

External positive character vacuums: these could include escape to a better place, a healthier world-view, a better relationship with someone and so on - things external to the character.

Internal positive character vacuums: these include things like a peace of mind a character would like to achieve, a state of fitness they want to reach, an emotion they'd like to express and so forth, part of the character's internal world.

External negative character vacuums: these could be things like declining health, insecurity in the character's environment, a hungry family or a forthcoming redundancy - real, external factors.

Internal negative character vacuums: including the fear of a future health problem, hunger, pain or personal depression or anxiety and so on - mainly psychological aspects.

Positive/negative, internal/external: master the recognition of character vacuums and vacuum generation becomes easy and predictable.

Positive character vacuums are not much used in fiction, except in stories for small children. Negative vacuums have more 'pull' as readers grow older.

Vacuums either pull the work toward the reader or the reader toward the work.

The job of the successful piece of fiction (made much easier by the observant writer) is to create vacuums that overlap with the vacuums of the reader and then magnify them.

Filling the vacuum produces a moment of fulfilment for the reader. A large vacuum being filled produces a bigger, more emotionally fulfilling effect.

The more creative and energetic the work is in creating and filling vacuums, the more successful it will be. If a work successfully fills a vacuum, the reader will either return to have more vacuums filled (even ones that he or she didn't realise were there!) or they will recommend other readers to come and read, through a contagion of vacuums.

Provide good adventure, effective tragedy, an enjoyable comedy, a powerful new thriller, a great children's story, a perfect new filmscript, or even lasting peace of mind and the reader who wanted it will return to you again and again. And they'll want their family and friends to come to you too. But what makes the adventure 'good' is vacuums; what makes the tragedy 'effective' is vacuums; what makes the comedy 'enjoyable' is vacuums, and so on. Specific examples of all of these things, with lots of detail, follow later.

But how exactly do you find or create vacuums?

Levels of Vacuum

Using these things - whether they were fully aware of them or not - successful works have grown into huge bestsellers.

Agatha Christie is the world's most successful crime writer with estimates of over two billion copies of her stories sold. How has she done this? *By creating and filling vacuums.*

The Harry Potter books became a commercial success stories that have made millions for their author, J. K. Rowling. How have they done this? *By finding and filling vacuums.*

Shakespeare and the other giants of literature have conquered the literary world over the centuries. How have they done this? *By finding and filling vacuums.*

You can probably think of countless examples, because there are countless examples:

Pride and Prejudice, Jane Eyre, Wuthering Heights, Tess Of The D'Urbervilles and other nineteenth century novels; *To The Lighthouse, A Passage to India, To Kill a Mockingbird* and other 20th century masterpieces; *The Lord of the Rings, Dune, Watership Down, The Lion, the Witch and the Wardrobe* and other works of fantasy and science fiction; modern films ranging from *Vertigo* in 1958 to *Captain America: The Winter Soldier* in 2014 - all these works of fiction have as their engine and beating heart the power of finding or creating vacuums of one kind or another and then filling them or purposefully leaving them empty. Some of these examples we will look at specifically in a later chapter.

You've been introduced to the four basic types of character vacuum above. But there are other categories of vacuum which you need to understand. These are the building blocks for character constructs and also for some plot vacuums, as you will see.

Some vacuums are inherent, automatic or basic. We have to eat, we all need shelter, we all have health requirements, we are all alive. Characters respond on a primal level when threatened with starvation, loss of homes, ill health or death. Think Dickens, think disaster movies, think vampire novels to a degree (vampirism being a form of death).

Some vacuums are not necessarily basic, but are so common that they are part of living: the need for companionship, the urge to be entertained and the desire to be educated are examples. These form the fabric of human society. Myriads of works of fiction exist to provide the sense of these to readers through carefully constructed characters.

In this group of vacuums, the mere fact that there are so many possibilities and variants opens the door to your success rather than restricts you. Examples of authors using vacuums of this kind are almost infinitely numerous: Jane's need for companionship in *Jane Eyre*; Pickwick's urge for justice in *The Pickwick Papers*; Anne's desire to be educated in *Anne of Green Gables*. A work that lacks these vacuums is going to seem hollow and shallow.

Then we get into the realms of the universal: things that characters don't need but might want, conveniences, comforts, luxuries, small things that just about everyone has lacked at some point of time or all the time.

Universal vacuums open the door to stories in a profoundly significant and almost all-embracing way, as we shall see.

This all becomes a little clearer when we put these levels of vacuums together with the reader, as in the following diagram.

The key thing to note here is:

All readers share universal vacuums.

That's why they're universal.

All readers at some point have suffered an inconvenience or discomfort. This means that they more readily grasp that level of vacuum when it is presented in a *character*.

You can create a potentially infinite number of convincing characters by creating and filling vacuums of these kinds.

World-famous authors have applied these levels of vacuums to build up the vacuum power in some of their leading characters. They do this by beginning with *universal vacuums* and underpinning them with

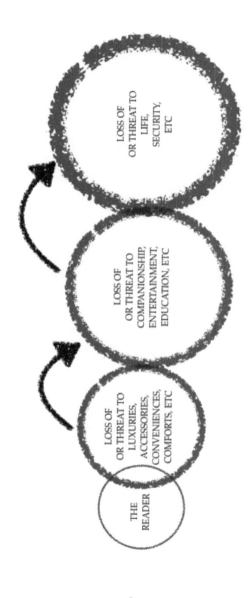

common vacuums and then the much more serious level of *basic vacuums*.

Basic vacuums, to do with life and death, shelter, health and security, are the foundation: on top of those, common vacuums like companionship, entertainment or education are overlaid. Sometimes there is no need for further vacuums; sometimes universal vacuums are interwoven into the construct to create a complex 'character'.

In *The Lord of the Rings*, as we have seen, Frodo loses home, friends and then suffers physically as he progresses through his adventure. The magnitude of the vacuum gets worse: he loses luxuries and accessories first, then later companionship, and, as his quest nears its end, he is threatened with pain, starvation and death. But he begins by being mildly inconvenienced by his neighbours.

Always the basic vacuums underpin the lesser ones.

The same kind of sequence is followed in almost all other tales: in *Watership Down*, by Richard Adams, the rabbit characters lose home and friends then later suffer pain and privation, always pursued by the shadow of death. In *Dune*, by Frank Herbert, protagonist Paul has to leave his home planet and loses shelter and companions before being threatened with death, all on the way to gaining wisdom. In the sequel *Dune Messiah* he even loses his eyesight. Jane in *Jane Eyre*, by Charlotte Brontë finds her situation progressively worsening and suffers greater and greater loss before her magical moment of fulfilment.

Master authors use these levels of vacuum whether they call them that or not - they are a scale of needs which readers recognise and respond to. The greater the need, the more its 'pulling power'. Some character vacuums are more complex than others, being woven of many kinds of vacuums, but all result in an increase in reader sympathy.

In *Tess Of The D'Urbervilles*, by Thomas Hardy, the character of Tess Durbeyfield, the novel's protagonist, is created by placing her in the path of destruction. Chief among the vacuums first presented is that of her immediate family, impoverished and uneducated. Tess, a beautiful, loyal young woman who lives with them in the village of Marlott, possesses a sense of responsibility and is committed to doing the best she can for her family, although her inexperience and lack of wise parenting leave her extremely vulnerable. Thus she gains character vacuums which attract reader sympathy like magnets.

Her life becomes complicated when her father discovers a link to the noble line of the d'Urbervilles. Tess is sent to work at the d'Urberville mansion, but slides further and further into misfortune after she becomes pregnant by Alec d'Urberville. The irony is that Tess and her family are not really related to this branch of the d'Urbervilles at all: Alec's father, a merchant named Simon Stokes, simply assumed the name. At the end of this sad tale, the gradually increasing vacuums that have been opened up in Tess's character are not filled, capturing Hardy's dark message about life and society.

In *A Passage to India*, by E. M. Forster, the similarly tragic heroine Adela Quested is seeking entertainment and education before her deeper, aching and more basic needs are touched upon in the Caves of Marabar, and her life falls apart as she goes on to suffer great physical pain and loss.

In *To Kill a Mockingbird*, by Harper Lee we are warned in the opening sentence that the child character Jem is going to suffer physical injury and then we are led through a deepening pattern of vacuums to find out how.

These patterns and correspondences are not a coincidence, they are a tool. In the 2014 film *Captain America: The Winter Soldier*, the protagonist Steve Rogers has the massive character vacuum of the loss of his entire time period mentioned in the opening scenes before plot vacuums pull the story along.

It doesn't matter what the medium is: characters in stories are constructed from the same basic material - emptinesses, needs, desires, of varying magnitudes.

So character vacuums are weaknesses, wounds, losses and deep needs on a scale of relative strengths: basics like shelter, health and security underpinning common needs like friendship or knowledge, overlaid with lesser needs like comforts or conveniences. Any significant character in any piece of fiction anywhere is composed of a mixture of these. Character vacuums are a vital tool in creating an effective work of fiction: well-rounded, fully biographied characters who have no burning needs of any kind are dead on the page.

It's almost as though the construct you're creating is made out of holes. The best and most memorable protagonists always are.

But how do character vacuums relate to the plot? Is a character vacuum enough to power an entire tale? What else moves the story forward?

Plot vacuums are of course going to get attention in due course. But before we look at them in detail, there's one particular type of character worth examining as he or she normally acts as a bridge between character and plot.

From Character to Plot

Initially, a story's central character usually has only a vague idea of real needs, as we have mentioned. They begin with universal vacuums, inconveniences, interruptions, losses of minor comforts. They may experience a common vacuum - the loss of a friend or family member or positive situation. Then, lo and behold, someone turns up to point out what the underlying basic vacuum is.

These characters, who have remarkably similar qualities and attributes across all of literature as we will examine in detail in a later chapter, can be summed up as *vacuum definers*, or *attention commanders*.

An 'attention commander' is a kind of character, who by reason of their position, behaviour or relationship to other characters in a story, is an authority figure or opinion leader for the central character construct who we are taking to be our protagonist. The mechanics of how this works are explained in a later section. For now, the thing to understand is that these senior characters *command attention* - they can direct where others look and what others notice.

In the examples above, this figure either appears and directs the protagonist towards the underlying basic vacuum that must be addressed.

In *The Lord of the Rings*, it's obviously Gandalf who points to the imminent loss of life and freedom across Middle Earth. In *Watership Down*, it's Fiver with his premonitions. In *Dune*, the vacuum definer is Paul's witch-like mother.

In *To Kill a Mockingbird*, the vacuum-defining old man is clearly Atticus; in *Captain America: The Winter Soldier*, it's Nick Fury.

Where these figures are weak or missing (though they are usually present in some form nevertheless) we have a different kind of tale with a bleaker conclusion.

Tess Of The D'Urbervilles has Tess Durbeyfield suffer so much largely because her father, who would normally be the vacuum-defining figure, is so weak; in *A Passage to India*, Adela lacks anyone to act as a definer for her, other than Fielding or the more remote Professor Godbole, after her life has already collapsed. That's why these stories belong to a different genre altogether, though they still follow the same principles.

Find the appropriate authority figure for your potential protagonist and he or she can be made aware of a vacuum that he or she didn't even know was there - which brings in the substance of the *plot*.

Remember, we are talking here about protagonists who initially know almost *nothing at all* about their real needs. They have few vacuums, external or internal, operating upon them in any way, or are trapped in a kind of 'vacuum stasis' at the beginning of the tale. They aren't looking for anything else, aren't necessarily thinking about anything else, are barely aware of anything else, except a sense of restlessness or some kind of universal vacuum.

The underlying basic need has to be put in front of them and made real.

It has to impinge upon them from 'outside', as it were. It has to hit them with authority, it has to grab their attention which is currently on other, lesser things, as in the following diagram.

Most writers through the ages use the archetype of the old man with a stick. You will immediately spot him as such in most of the stories we have touched upon: Gandalf the wizard, Obi Wan Kenobi the Jedi, Dumbledore the wizard, and so on.

This character is slightly less obvious in many other works, as we have seen: Professor Godbole in *A Passage to India*, Atticus in *To Kill a Mockingbird*, Jaggers in *Great Expectations*, the wizard in *The Wizard of Oz*, Clarence the angel in *It's a Wonderful Life*, Doc Smith

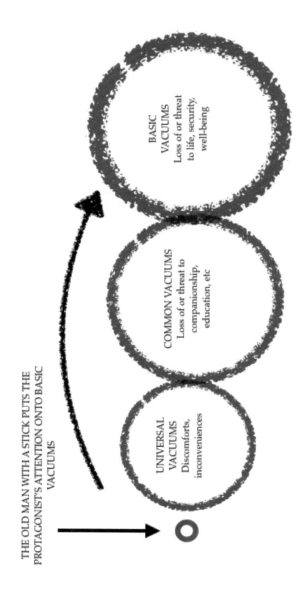

BASIC VACUUMS
Loss of or threat to life, security, well-being

COMMON VACUUMS
Loss of or threat to companionship, education, etc

UNIVERSAL VACUUMS
Discomforts, inconveniences

THE OLD MAN WITH A STICK PUTS THE PROTAGONIST'S ATTENTION ONTO BASIC VACUUMS

in *Back to the Future*, Nick Fury in *Captain America: The Winter Soldier*, and *The Avengers* and so on. In all of these works, and in many more, easily recognisable or not, the figure of the old man - who usually has a stick or object of power with him - fulfils much the same function: he informs the protagonist (and therefore the reader) of the nature of the basic vacuum which is central to the story.

They can be good or bad, positive or negative. Jaggers motives in *Great Expectations* seem totally different to Clarence's in *It's a Wonderful Life*. All that really matters is that *attention can be commanded by them*.

When they speak, people listen. When they endorse, people 'pay attention'. When they point out an underlying basic vacuum, it sparks the plot into life.

Suddenly, protagonists experience an awareness of such a thing as a basic vacuum - because someone they innately respect, even if only a little, has said that they favour something, need something, have to draw our attention to something. A need, however slight, is awakened and a real plot vacuum is born. Encourage it to grow and the character begins to move and the reader begins to develop momentum through the work.

You'll learn much more about characters and how they relate to plots later. First, you have to see how combinations of the vacuums you have learned about so far create the wide variety of fiction that you see around you in novels, plays, films and short stories.

Vacuums interact with each other to create different effects. Firstly, they create the four basic genres of fiction itself; secondly, they create a set of characters who are recognisable across the whole range of fiction.

Chapter Four:
The Wheel of Fiction

You now know what's been wrong with the characters you've devised who just don't seem to work. And what's right about the characters who seem alive. You now know what motivates characters, to varying degrees, across the whole range of fiction.

This knowledge alone should have moved you to the right along the Spectrum of Fiction above.

Characters who have vacuums - basic, common, or universal - enable readers to more directly experience the text.

Obviously, in the pursuit of your goals as a fiction writer, other basics have to be in place. You have to be writing in the same language as your prospective readership. An entire novel in French will communicate exactly nothing to a non-French-speaking person.

Above words and their order, though, lies a layer of what we might call 'established reader expectations' which fiction writers tap into as soon as they put pen to paper (or finger to keyboard). This overlying pattern or web is alive, shifting, interweaving itself all the time. And what animates it is *vacuums*.

These established reader expectations fall into four broad categories. They've been called 'genres' before, but that word can be misleading - for now, think of them as templates containing certain patterns of vacuums:

• The set of expectations involving a somewhat-sane protagonist, not overwhelmed by his or her character vacuums, who moves through a relatively ordered world to confront and ultimately triumph over an antagonist. This is the set of stories called 'Epics' and this is the most commonly used template and the one upon which the others rest.

• The set of expectations involving a more and more insane protagonist, gradually ruined by his or her character vacuums, who moves through a relatively ordered world but who, due to a growing internal imbalance, fails to triumph. This is the set of stories called 'Tragedies'.

• The set of expectations involving a more-or-less insane or overwhelmed protagonist who moves through a disordered world full of vacuums, ending up defeated and isolated. This is the set of stories called 'Ironies'.

• The set of expectations involving a somewhat-sane or recovering protagonist who moves through a disordered world to ultimately join or re-join an ordered society. This is the set of stories called 'Comedies'.

Epic Stories

These four broad categories can be placed on a 'Wheel of Fiction'. In the top right hand quarter, let's place everything we've learned so far about our most common type of story model, that associated with 90% of the stories we generally encounter. This is the 'Summer' quarter. As we look further into the four categories, we will see exactly what plot vacuums it uses and how.

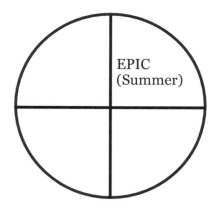

These stories, feature a classic hero and following a classic pattern:

• the protagonist is usually a young boy or servant (loss of status creating a vacuum)

• he is missing at least one parent (creating a common vacuum)

• he is being brought up by a close family member or social superior

• he encounters an old man with a stick (the 'vacuum definer' as described above)

• the old man orientates him to the antagonist, opening up the basic vacuum of the story

• a journey or quest commences, usually physical, pulled forward by this basic vacuum

• the protagonist is scarred, wounded or otherwise damaged before or during this journey - all individual character vacuums

• the protagonist acquires a comic companion who becomes pivotal in the journey

• the protagonist also often meets a female companion

• there is also a warrior king - an older companion with particular characteristics

• the protagonist often has a shadow - a character similar in many ways to the protagonist but often a kind of opposite

• a war between 'good' and 'evil' is taking place as a backdrop to the story - this is the basic vacuum, the threat to life or health, which is the dominating narrative force

• eventually, the protagonist meets and defeats the antagonist, usually at personal cost (another character vacuum), and usually by finding a close familial or psychological connection between them (about which more later)

• the protagonist transcends the world in which he has lived, leaving companions behind.

There are obvious examples which follow this template exactly: *The Lord of the Rings*, the *Star Wars* films, the Harry Potter books, the King Arthur stories, and so forth. But other stories that might not spring to mind immediately but which hug this template closely include:

Dune, by Frank Herbert
Watership Down, by Richard Adams
The Lion, the Witch and the Wardrobe, by C. S. Lewis
The Wind in the Willows, by Kenneth Grahame
The Hobbit, by J. R. R. Tolkien
Toy Story, 1995
The Wizard of Oz, 1939
Captain America: The Winter Soldier, 2014

There are many, many others. I'm sure you can think of a few. They cover a range of forms and media, but all possess the above points in common.

Though this template seems to be a story with which we are very familiar, appearing constantly in various forms, repeatedly reinvented around us through Hollywood, in the bestseller lists, on television and elsewhere, though other writers have traced some or most of the patterns, no one seems to ask *why* it works or how come it is repeated almost without deviation, time and time again. Only by understanding vacuums can we understand the principles behind the template.

Tragic Stories

Following the four categories described above, this template has three other major variations.

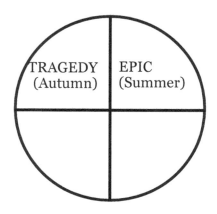

In tragic stories, these are the repeating elements:

• the protagonist is usually a mature warrior figure, seemingly possessed of no inner vacuums at first

• he is missing at least one parent (a common vacuum)

• he is often, but not exclusively, a social superior

• he experiences loss or defeat early on (another vacuum)

• he encounters an old man with a stick, often a foolish figure, who orientates him to the antagonist and basic vacuum, but this is often ignored or misinterpreted

• a journey or quest commences, usually based on an internal, psychological vacuum

• the protagonist is scarred, wounded or otherwise damaged before or during this journey, usually psychologically

• the protagonist loses a comic companion

• the protagonist also often loses a female companion

• there is also a warrior king - an older companion with particular characteristics

• the protagonist often has a shadow - a character similar in many ways to the protagonist but often a kind of opposite

• a war between 'good' and 'evil' is taking place as a backdrop to the story, but the definitions of what is 'good' and what is 'evil' are blurring

• eventually, the protagonist meets but is defeated by an antagonist, usually resulting in the protagonist's death and usually by finding a close familial or psychological connection between them.

The most typical examples of this type of story, normally called Tragedies, are the Shakespearian plays *Macbeth*, *King Lear* and *Othello*. Other examples of stories with tragic overtones include: *Wuthering Heights*, by Emily Brontë; the *Harry Potter* series (if seen as the story of Severus Snape) by J. K. Rowling: the complete *Star Wars* film series (if seen as the story of Darth Vader).

Tragedy is a relatively rare genre in today's culture, for reasons which will become clear later. This quarter is called the 'Autumn' quarter.

Ironic Stories

Things in fiction can be worse than death, and the bottom left quarter begins with death and gets worse. This quarter, the Ironic segment, takes the same model we started with and flips it even further, into 'Winter'.

You will note some subtle changes from the original 'Summer' template, usually mirror images:

• the protagonist is often (but not exclusively) a young girl or servant

• she is missing at least one parent

• she is being brought up by a close family member or social superior

• she encounters an old man with a stick

• the old man orientates her to the antagonist, opening up the basic vacuum of the story, but as this is an Irony his advice is often twisted or duplicitous

• a journey or quest commences, usually psychological, pulled forward by the basic vacuum

• the protagonist is scarred, wounded or otherwise damaged before or during this journey - an individual vacuum which is usually, in Irony, quite central and overwhelming

• the protagonist acquires a comic companion who becomes pivotal in the journey

• the protagonist also often meets a male companion

• there is also a warrior king - an older companion with particular characteristics, who is, in the Irony quarter, often seriously flawed himself

• the protagonist often has a shadow - a character similar in many ways to the protagonist but often an opposite

• a war between 'good' and 'evil' is taking place as a backdrop to the story but the definitions are so confused as to be opaque to the reader

• eventually, the protagonist degenerates and fails, usually finding a close familial or psychological connection between herself and the antagonist

• the protagonist leaves the world in which she has lived, often in shame, leaving companions behind.

Allowing for differences in the gender of the protagonist, examples here include *Great Expectations*, the films *Brazil* and *Fight Club*, *1984*, *An Inspector Calls* and many others including:

Tess Of The D'Urbervilles, by Thomas Hardy
A Passage to India, by E.M. Forster
Great Expectations, by Charles Dickens
Captain Corelli's Mandolin, by Louis de Bernieres
Animal Farm, by George Orwell

Pulp Fiction, 1994
Blade Runner, 1982

For reasons which should become apparent later, our present culture produces more of the Irony genre than has been seen in previous generations.

It is the quarter of the horror story, the dark detective thriller, the unsolved mystery, the twisted and unending nightmare. It is the quarter where things which would be neatly resolved in the Epic or even Tragic quarters are left unresolved, often explicitly. Whereas the Epic apex is one of enlightenment and release, here at the nadir of the circle waits only despair and eternal captivity. Horror as an established genre belongs in this quarter.

One of the key features of Ironies is that things get a little 'mixed up': time is often out of sequence (as in *Pulp Fiction*), characters have split personalities (as in *Fight Club*) and reality can take on the colour of nightmares (as in *Brazil*).

What this boils down to is this:

In Ironies, vacuums are intentionally left empty.

Frankly, things get so bad at the bottom of the circle that the only response likely to create any kind of upswing is laughter. Like a really bad day when everything that could possibly go wrong actually does go wrong, leaving us exasperated in the extreme, we can get to the point where reality just seems absurd. Art movements based on the absurd predominated in the early part of the twentieth century as people tried to come to terms with living in an Ironic age.

Comic Stories

Oddly enough, though, laughter at the absurdity pushes us over the line into the final quarter of the circle: Comedy, or 'Spring'.

Again, the template 'flips', but now everything is on an upward swing once more.

• the protagonist is often a young girl or servant

• she is missing at least one parent

• she is being brought up by a close family member or social superior

• she encounters an old man with a stick, often a foolish figure

• the old man orientates her to a comic nemesis, opening up the basic vacuum of the story, but his advice or input is often comedically exaggerated in some way

• a journey or quest commences, usually physical again, pulled forward by the basic vacuum

• the protagonist is scarred, wounded or otherwise damaged before or during this journey - an individual vacuum which is usually, in Comedy, light and laughable in some way, a quirk or foible rather than a serious wound

• the protagonist acquires a comic companion who becomes pivotal in the journey

• the protagonist also often meets a male companion

• there is also a warrior king - an older companion with particular characteristics, who, in the Comedy quarter, sometimes becomes a love interest

• the protagonist often has a shadow - a character similar in many ways to the protagonist but often an opposite

• a war between 'good' and 'evil' is taking place as a backdrop to the story but the battle is played out as a farce

• eventually, the protagonist comes to some kind of resolution, often marrying the antagonist

• the protagonist rejoins the society in which she lives.

Often the hero or heroine remains celibate or virginal. Disguise, cross-gendering and mixed roles play a large part in traditional comedies and farces.

Thousands of examples exist: Shakespeare's comedies, Restoration farces, comedies of manners, television sit-coms, the list is probably endless. This quarter includes what is normally referred to as 'romances'.

And so we literally come full circle, back into the restored and ordered world of the Epic. Specific examples of Comedy include:

Winnie the Pooh, by A. A. Milne
Jane Eyre, by Charlotte Brontë
Persuasion, by Jane Austen
Emma, by Jane Austen
Anne Of Green Gables, by L. M. Montgomery
A Christmas Carol, by Charles Dickens
It's a Wonderful Life, 1946
Groundhog Day, 1993
Back to the Future, 1985

These four templates - Epic, Tragic, Ironic and Comic - form the foundation of all story-telling.

Of course, there are subtle gradations or overlaps sometimes. Some stories, while holding the shape of a Summer quarter, start to shade towards Autumn. These could be called 'Autumn Epics' and *The Lord of the Rings* might be better described as one of them.

Similarly, a story might be at its heart following an Epic pattern, but be light-hearted and even frivolous in tone. So we get a 'Spring Epic' like *The Princess Bride*, for example.

There are plenty of examples these days of heroic adventure tales which are overcast with a sense of horror or gloom - most modern thrillers fall into this grouping. The hero still triumphs but the mood is downcast - for example, the films *Alien* and *Aliens*, along with *The*

Bourne Identity and its sequels, or novels such as *To Kill a Mockingbird* in which racism is still triumphing but the protagonist learns real wisdom. These are 'Winter Epics'.

Can one have a 'Spring Tragedy', a blend of comedy and seriousness that captures both seasons? Some of Shakespeare's works possibly fall into this grouping, such as *Twelfth Night* or *Much Ado About Nothing*.

Modern culture is Ironic in nature - thus we can have many shades of Winter in our fiction, even when it is ultimately light-hearted. Dark Comedies such as the film *Dr. Strangelove*, or the TV series *Red Dwarf* or Joseph Heller's novel *Catch-22* are what could be called 'Spring Ironies' or 'Winter Comedies'. George R. R. Martin's *A Song of Fire and Ice* series, made into the television series *Game of Thrones*, is clearly a Winter Epic.

With these four fundamental categories and their shadings, the entire world of fiction is covered. Detailed case studies showing how these templates are used in famous works of fiction come in later chapters. But with these templates in mind, you should have seen past the first 'veil' of fiction and realised that every single story you have ever read is using identical patterns to lead you through to some kind of parallel conclusion.

Epics always end in victory for the 'right' side; Tragedies always end with the death of the protagonist, portrayed as a sad loss of potential; Ironies always end in a kind of introverted nightmare; Comedies always end with reunion or marriage or both.

If you want to create a happy, upbeat effect, the categories of Comedy and Epic give you your first broad guidelines; if you want to create a more introverted, downbeat effect, then Tragedy or Irony are your tools.

More specifically, if your story is about a conflict between 'good' and 'evil' in which 'good' triumphs, then Epic gives you your basic layout. If you, on the other hand, want to tell a tale of loss, folly and misdirected intentions, which results in the wasteful death of the protagonist, then Tragedy is your template.

'Surely not?' you may respond. 'If I just use the template, surely I'm telling the same story as everyone else? What happened to originality or creativity?'

It's a big question. But the blunt fact is that *any successful piece of fiction uses one of these templates to one degree or another*. And the strange truth is that the more successful the work, the more closely the template has been followed.

Rather than finding thousands of departures from this statement, you will soon see how authors use vacuums in remarkably similar ways in almost every story you will be able to think of.

Vacuums in 'To Kill a Mockingbird'

Let's take a closer look at *To Kill a Mockingbird*, the classic American tale by Harper Lee that some call the greatest novel of the 20th century.

This novel is a 'Winter Epic' in that it follows the basic pattern of an Epic, but with Ironic overtones.

Set in the sleepy Alabama town of Maycomb in the 1930s, Lee's famous story of Scout Finch who lives with her brother, Jem, and their widowed father, Atticus, has firmly established itself as a modern classic. Our first sign of an Ironic overtone is the fact that the story is narrated by an older Scout - the whole tale is actually a 'flashback'. However, the narration is done with such expertise that we are deceived into thinking that we are in fact in Scout's childlike mind most of the time.

Maycomb is enduring the Great Depression, but Atticus is a lawyer and the Finch family is well off in comparison to the rest of the town. One summer, Jem and Scout meet a boy named Dill, who has come to live in their neighbourhood for the summer, and the three of them act out stories together. Dill quickly becomes fascinated with the old house on their street called the Radley Place, owned by Mr. Nathan Radley, whose brother, Arthur (nicknamed Boo) has lived there for years without ever going outside.

As a part of many adventures, during which the tone and themes of the story are established, the children begin to act out the story of Boo Radley, but Atticus puts a stop to this, urging the children to try to see life from another person's perspective before making judgements. Nevertheless, their fascination and involvement with the Radley household continues, despite the fact that Boo is never actually seen by any of them at this stage.

Halfway through the novel, the direction of the plot changes and we become embroiled in a case which has deeply disturbed Maycomb's racist white community. Atticus is appointed to and agrees to defend a black man named Tom Robinson, who has been accused of raping a white woman. This means that Jem and Scout are subjected to racist abuse from other children, and this prompts Atticus's stuffy sister, Alexandra, to come to live with the Finches the next summer. When the accused man is placed in the local jail, Atticus confronts the lynch mob the night before the trial. Scout recognises one of the men, and her innocence shames him into dispersing the mob.

At the trial itself, the children sit with the black inhabitants of the town, but, although Atticus provides clear evidence that the accusers, Mayella Ewell and her father, Bob, are lying, the all-white jury convicts him. Tom later tries to escape from prison and is shot to death. Jem's faith in justice is badly shaken, and he lapses into depression, but when Bob Ewell, bitter about being made a fool of in front of the town, finally attacks Jem and Scout as they walk home from a town pageant, Boo Radley at last emerges and intervenes, saving the children. Ewell is fatally stabbed during the struggle, and the sheriff, in order to protect Boo, insists that Ewell tripped over a tree root and fell on his own knife. Boo then disappears once more into the Radley house.

Initially, it reads as a modern novel, quite different to the Epic pattern we have been looking at. The Epic model, to refresh your memory, looks like this:

• the protagonist is usually a young boy or servant

• he is missing at least one parent

• he is being brought up by a close family member or social superior

• he encounters an old man with a stick

• the old man orientates him to the antagonist, opening up the basic vacuum of the story

• a journey or quest commences, usually physical, pulled forward by the basic vacuum

• the protagonist is scarred, wounded or otherwise damaged before or during this journey - an individual vacuum

• the protagonist acquires a comic companion who becomes pivotal in the journey

• the protagonist also often meets a female companion

• there is also a warrior king - an older companion with particular characteristics

• the protagonist often has a shadow - a character similar in many ways to the protagonist but often an opposite

• a war between 'good' and 'evil' is taking place as a backdrop to the story

• eventually, the protagonist meets and defeats the antagonist, usually at cost, and usually by finding a close familial or psychological connection between them

• the protagonist transcends the world in which he has lived, leaving companions behind.

Remember, there are going to be Ironic overtones in *To Kill a Mockingbird*, so some of these points will be a little 'mixed up', but the basics are all there:

The protagonist is Scout - but she is the shadow of her brother, Jem, a young boy. Scout is not especially feminine - most girls in Scout's position would be wearing dresses and learning manners, but thanks to Atticus's parenting, she wears overalls and learns to climb trees with Jem and Dill. The children are missing their mother, who has died some years before the commencement of the narrative. Scout and Jem are brought up by their father and later assisted by Aunt Alexandra, who considers herself to be a social superior. The 'old man with a stick' in this case is Atticus himself - his stick is the rifle with which he is an expert sharpshooter. It is Atticus who orientates the children to the 'antagonist' which in this novel is the racist ignorance personified in Bob Ewell. The basic vacuum of the story is the violent, racist hypocrisy of Ewell which threatens the children with death.

The journey or quest commences, in this case partly psychological as we see in the court case scenes, and partly physical, as we see in Chapter 27's walk with Jem ('Thus began our longest journey together.')

The very first sentence of the novel establishes that Jem is wounded before the story gets going, creating an individual vacuum which draws us towards him as a character.

Scout and Jem acquire a comic companion, Dill, who becomes pivotal in their journey: it is he who prompts them to investigate Boo Radley. Scout also has child-like romantic connections with Dill, an Ironic twist on the 'protagonist also often meets a female companion' point.

There is also a warrior king - an older companion with particular characteristics. Given the Ironic overtones, this is Boo Radley himself, who physically rescues the children from death.

Jem, as protagonist, has Scout as his shadow; a war between 'good' and 'evil' is taking place as a backdrop to the story, in the race relations of Maycomb.

Eventually, the protagonist meets and defeats the antagonist, at cost (in this case a brutal injury), and by finding a close familial or psychological connection between them - in this case, readers can make their own comparisons between Atticus as a father and Ewell as a father.

It's an Ironic oddity that Jem, the protagonist, 'transcends the world in which he has lived, leaving companions behind' at the end because he never recovers consciousness in the narrative after his injury. However, whether Scout is a companion or the protagonist, she transcends the normality in which she was brought up by the last pages of the novel. She feels as though she can finally imagine what life was like for the mysterious Boo: he has become human to her at last. Scout comes to understand her father's advice about sympathy with others and demonstrates that her experiences with prejudice have not spoiled her faith in humanity.

Uncannily, the basic storyline of *To Kill a Mockingbird* has satisfied more than 90% of the criteria associated with the template we outlined previously - the same template which fits the tales of King Arthur, the epics of the Middle Ages, *The Lord of the Rings* and the *Star Wars* films as well as hundreds of other stories. No particular effort to stretch or modify the pattern in any way has been made - the book just naturally falls into its mould.

The fact that the book so closely follows our established pattern takes nothing away from it: it is still about the moral nature of human beings, whether people are essentially good or evil, the transition from a perspective of childhood innocence to a more adult perspective. Hatred, prejudice, and ignorance are shown very effectively to pose a threat to the innocent: Tom Robinson and Boo Radley are innocent but are destroyed in some way. The novel is deservedly a classic.

And so Harper Lee gets her point across, by using the Ironic template coupled with elements of the Epic, exactly per the fundamentals we have described.

She wanted to bring about a feeling of enlightenment about the world, almost a purely intellectual idea. Why didn't she simply write a treatise on racism in the Deep South and hand that out to people? Why go to all the trouble of creating an effect on a reader through a story? Because in that way she reaches many more readers and impinges much more subtly upon them.

Fiction is that set of procedures or tools used by writers to obtain emotional commitment from readers in order to create specific effects upon them.

To Kill a Mockingbird, like all successful works of fiction, weaves a spell: Harper Lee tries, as a writer, to create an effect or set of effects on readers without them knowing particularly what she is doing. By the time you get to the end of the novel, its overall effect has 'snuck up on you'.

Lee has used the category of Epic, overlaid with Irony, to make her general point. She has used the constructs we have call 'characters' to attract and hold our attention. She has devised a series of vacuums which we are accustomed to calling a 'plot' which actually works, drawing our attention along with vacuum after vacuum until her goal is achieved.

She has successfully pulled off a trick: the trick called 'fiction'.

Vacuums in 'Macbeth'

If you need another example, let's look at a famous Tragedy, Shakespeare's *Macbeth,* recollecting that the main points of a Tragedy are:

• the protagonist is usually a mature warrior figure

• he is missing at least one parent

• he is often, but not exclusively, a social superior

• he experiences defeat early on

• he encounters an old man with a stick, often a foolish figure, who orientates him to the basic vacuum, but this is often ignored

• a journey or quest commences, usually based on an internal, psychological vacuum

• the protagonist is scarred, wounded or otherwise damaged before or during this journey, usually psychologically

• the protagonist loses a comic companion

• the protagonist also often loses a female companion

• there is also a warrior king - an older companion with particular characteristics

• the protagonist often has a shadow - a character similar in many ways to the protagonist but often an opposite

• a war between 'good' and 'evil' is taking place as a backdrop to the story, but the definitions of what is 'good' and what is 'evil' are blurring

• eventually, the protagonist meets but is defeated by an antagonist, usually resulting in the protagonist's death and usually by finding a close familial or psychological connection between them.

Macbeth tells the tale of a Scottish warrior who, encountering a triad of sinister witches, appears to succumb to their prophecies that he will become King of Scotland by murdering the current incumbent and taking the throne, which he then feels he has to protect through a series of brutal psychotic actions. Needless to say, he wins no friends and declines, losing allies and even his murderous wife, before being killed by the man he had feared the most. Justice is eventually restored in Scotland, but not without a feeling of profound disturbance in the order of things.

Macbeth himself is a mature warrior figure whose bravery in battle is much vaunted at the beginning of the play; as far as we know he is an orphan; he is certainly a social superior when the play opens, but he experiences loss when King Duncan appoints his own son heir to the throne rather than the battle-triumphant Macbeth.

We glimpse an old man with a stick, who orientates us to the disorder in the world, but this is ignored. It is the witches who indicate the basic psychological vacuum in Macbeth: his terrible ambition.

Macbeth's journey or quest is certainly an internal, psychological vacuum as he hallucinates and torments himself into further psychotic episodes. Evidence in the text suggests that he is already psychologically damaged before or during this journey.

We even briefly glimpse a comic companion (the porter) though the play does not dwell on comic moments. Macbeth loses his female companion, Lady Macbeth, to suicide.

The warrior king - an older companion with particular characteristics - is an interesting one in Tragedy. It could be argued that the protagonist becomes the warrior king - Macbeth certainly does.

He has a shadow - a character similar in many ways to himself but in some ways an opposite: Banquo.

A war between 'good' and 'evil' is taking place as a backdrop to the story, but the definitions of what is 'good' and what is 'evil' are certainly blurred.

Eventually, Macbeth meets but is defeated by Macduff, resulting in the former's death. As to the suggestion of a close familial or psychological connection between them, there is a sub-text in the play to do with the possibility that Macbeth's inner vacuum or motivation has to do with children or his lack of them - and much is made of Macduff's birth and his children.

Again, a Tragedy has fallen almost completely in line with our template, without any particular effort to 'squeeze' it into place.

Vacuums in 'Pride and Prejudice'

Let's look at a Comedy or 'romance'. Jane Austen's *Pride and Prejudice* is a perfect prototype.

Here are the points for the Comedy template again:

• the protagonist is often a young girl or servant

• she is missing at least one parent

• she is being brought up by a close family member or social superior

• she encounters an old man with a stick, often a foolish figure

• the old man orientates her to a comic nemesis, opening up the basic vacuum of the story, but his advice is often comedically exaggerated in some way

• a journey or quest commences, usually physical again, pulled forward by the basic vacuum

• the protagonist is scarred, wounded or otherwise damaged before or during this journey - an individual vacuum which is usually, in Comedy, light and laughable in some way, a quirk or foible rather than a serious wound.

• the protagonist acquires a comic companion who becomes pivotal in the journey

• the protagonist also often meets a male companion

• there is also a warrior king - an older companion with particular characteristics, who, in the Comedy quarter, sometimes becomes a love interest

• the protagonist often has a shadow - a character similar in many ways to the protagonist but often an opposite

• a war between 'good' and 'evil' is taking place as a backdrop to the story but the battle is played out as a farce

• eventually, the protagonist comes to some kind of resolution, often marrying the antagonist

• the protagonist rejoins the society in which she lives.

In *Pride and Prejudice*, our protagonist is Elizabeth Bennett, a young girl, one of a group of unmarried daughters whose position is threatened in society due to their lack of marital relations.

It can't be said that she is 'missing at least one parent', though her mother's silliness could partly qualify her as missing but she does encounter an old man with a stick, her father, often a foolish figure, but possessed in this novel of an ironic wisdom. Her father orientates Lizzy to her comic nemesis, in effect opening up the main vacuum of the story, but his advice is often comedically exaggerated in some way.

Lizzy's journey or quest commences, usually physical again, in this case culminating in the search for her recalcitrant sister who has eloped. Lizzy is scarred, wounded or otherwise damaged before or during this journey by the rejections of Mr. Darcy, who fulfils the requirement of a male companion and a 'warrior king' who becomes a love interest.

Mr. Collins also steps in to tick the 'comic figure' box too.

Lizzy has two shadows - character similar in many ways to herself but often opposites - her friend Charlotte (who ends up marrying the comically repulsive Mr. Collins) and her sister Jane.

The war between 'good' and 'evil' here is the battle between Pride and Prejudice in various forms, personified at different times in a range of characters and events.

Eventually, as our template predicts, Lizzy marries her 'antagonist' Mr Darcy and all is well, as the marriage enables the whole Bennett family to safely rejoin the society which had threatened to expel them.

So various works of fiction, we can conclude, follow various but very similar patterns. Recognising that will change the way you view books, films, TV programmes and any other fictitious construction from now on. But these things have been observed to some degree before and are not entirely new, even though the level of detail in the similarities is often missed. The real questions are 'Why?' and 'How?': 'Why do authors employ these well-tried patterns?' and 'How do these patterns actually work? What drives them?'

The answers boil down to some even deeper simplicities, and open the door to an understanding of plot vacuums. But before we examine the various specific kinds of plot vacuums that exist, we need to examine a few more basics about characters.

Chapter Five:
The Protagonist and Company

If we are correct that, as we suggest above, the main purpose of fiction is to communicate something to the reader, to create some kind of effect, then along with writing in the same language as the reader (coupled with basic spelling and universal grammar) we have these 'patterns of expectation' or templates to assist in getting that message across.

As we have seen, character vacuums are universally used to attract the reader. Even an 'unattractive' character like an antagonist has character vacuums.

Then, when it comes to types of plot, happy or positive messages use Comedy or Epic; unhappy or negative messages use Tragedy or Irony.

If you like, rather than write a simple message on a piece of paper and hand it to readers, fiction writers have developed over many centuries a system of 'codes' so that readers know basically which of their emotional needs will be served. Someone in the mood for an uplifting experience will know through certain signs that such-and-such a work offers them a comic or epic experience; those in a more thoughtful or downbeat mood will spot the indications that certain works will provide them with certain outcomes more suited to their tastes at that time.

These templates are recognised in much the same way as the letters of the alphabet are recognised, words are recognised or grammar is recognised.

If you as a fiction writer are not interested in serving a reader's needs. but simply want to write 'from your own head', disregarding the reader entirely, then chances are that, just as you still use letters, words and grammar, you will still strike one of these patterns taking shape in your fiction. Chances are slender that you will perfectly match each and every point of the template that you need to be successful with readers, though. More normally, a writer needs to know these points by heart in the same way that a musician needs to practice certain musical forms to have any hope of capturing a listener's ear.

Let's assume that you do want to communicate some kind of effect, intellectual, emotional, spiritual or some combination, to a set of readers. Then you will want to become familiar with these templates and put into them your own ideas and images.

Where do you start?

We've been taught in and out of school that a character is a fictitious personality who, to be successful, must appear to be 'as lifelike as possible'.

We've been similarly taught that a plot, in order to attract readers, must contain 'conflict'.

We've been taught that any work of fiction has to have at least three acts with a dramatic curve heading upwards to a climax, followed by a denouement that completes the tale.

We get taught these things in schools, even in writing classes for adults; we read about these things in critical reviews or fan letters; we are drowned in the terminology that comes with these things, particularly the words 'drama', 'conflict', 'verisimilitude' and 'climax'.

All of these ideas are at best only partial truths.

Similarities in Protagonists

We've already examined the thing that we know by the term 'character' and found that many protagonists are almost identical. Frodo the halfling protagonist in *The Lord of the Rings*, is an orphan who is stabbed, stung and loses a finger in the course of his journey; Paul Atreides in the science-fiction classic *Dune*, by Frank Herbert, loses his father and is later struck blind in his adventures; Will, the child protagonist, loses his mother and then his fingers in the second of the *His Dark Materials* trilogy by Philip Pullman; Jem, one of the child protagonists of *To Kill a Mockingbird*, by Harper Lee, having already lost his mother, has his arm broken as part of his journey.

Jane, the eponymous heroine of *Jane Eyre*, by Charlotte Brontë, Heathcliff, the wayward protagonist of *Wuthering Heights*, by Emily Brontë, Pip, the child hero of *Great Expectations*, by Charles Dickens, Anne in *Anne Of Green Gables*, by L.M. Montgomery, and Harry in *Harry Potter And The Philosopher's Stone*, by J.K. Rowling are all orphans and are all wounded either physically or emotionally on their journeys. Harry receives his scar while still a baby.

In the film world, examples are again too numerous to mention: George Bailey in Frank Capra's classic *It's a Wonderful Life*, loses his father and is afflicted with deafness in one ear; Luke Skywalker thinks that he is an orphan and even loses the relatives who were raising him in *Star Wars: A New Hope*.

Fiction is quite a brutal world.

That heroes of tales are often orphans is nothing new, strange though it may seem to look at rawly like this. But the question that few seem to ask is '*Why* are so many of these protagonists orphans? *Why* are so many of them savagely wounded in some way in their stories?'

One obvious answer is 'to gain sympathy from the reader.' Orphans are immediately sympathetic figures for most readers. Wounds and scars increase that sense of sympathy and wanting to help, increasing the identification with the star of the story.

But as we have seen, it is actually even simpler than that.

The loss of one parent or both creates a *vacuum*. The loss of appendages, limbs, or health creates *vacuums*. Vacuums attract attention. By robbing their protagonists of the standard support of one or more of these things, successful fiction writers immediately attract reader attention. This has very little to do with verisimilitude - when you think about it, in real life not that many people are actually orphans or are brutalised in the way that most protagonists are. It has everything to do with *vacuums*.

The first law of character development is: create vacuums.

Vacuums 'suck' attention from the reader.

If this is done skilfully enough, the reader will stick like glue to what we are used to calling a 'protagonist'. And that more or less defines what a protagonist is: the point at which a story most sticks the reader's attention.

A protagonist is defined as that constructed figure who attracts and holds the most reader attention.

The usual method of doing that involves robbing a child of its parents. We don't need to know much about this child-figure at all - normally protagonists are remarkably sketchily drawn when closely examined. The important thing in terms of establishing them with the reader is *to create a powerful enough vacuum around one figure.*

Frodo in *The Lord of the Rings*, loses his parents in a boating accident. There is remarkably little else that we know about him, including very little physical description. He responds fairly ordinarily to the situations presented to him in the tale - he is anxious when one would expect him to be anxious, afraid when it would be appropriate for him to be afraid, and so on. In other words, there's nothing particularly interesting about him as such. What we pick up on and follow is that he is losing things: as we have seen, he has to give up his home, his country, and his friends in the first part of the book. In other words, *the vacuum gets bigger around him* as the story progresses. Soon he loses his mentor Gandalf, his companions, his protector Aragorn and then parts of his body. And of course he is being continually plagued by the Ring, which constantly tempts him with the vacuum of invisibility and more sinister things. (The Ring is a marvellous fictive device for linking the protagonist with the basic vacuum - in the case, the destruction of the entire world through Sauron, the Dark Lord.)

Just when our attention might begin to drift from him as the protagonist onto his more amusing companions Sam or even Pippin or Merry, Frodo is stabbed on Weathertop by a Morgul-knife. His drifting in and out of full consciousness from that point, far from making him less interesting, actually serves to guarantee to the reader that he *is* the protagonist - he is definitely the vacuum point which sticks our attention the most. We don't hear much from him in some chapters; the dialogue and direction falls to others - but that doesn't matter. We know as readers that our 'hero', our central character, is Frodo. Why?

He is the one with the most vacuums.

Gandalf says of Frodo that 'He may become like a glass filled with a clear light for eyes to see that can.'

As the story goes on, it is Frodo who takes on the burden of the Ring though he does 'not know the way' (another vacuum); it is Frodo who acts as our point of interest, even on the hill of Amon Hen when the battle between the will of Sauron and another voice from afar that speaks in Frodo's head is fought on his almost neutral 'canvas'.

> Then as a flash from some other power there came to his mind another thought: *Take it off! Take it off! Fool, take it off! Take off the Ring!* The two powers strove in him, for a moment, perfectly balanced between their piercing points, he writhed, tormented. Suddenly he was aware of himself again. Frodo, neither the Voice nor the Eye: free to choose, and with one remaining instant with to do so. He took the ring off his finger.

Later, when he has again given up all the rest of his companions and journeyed closer to Mordor, he gathers to himself the character of Gollum, who could be described as a living vacuum, a creature who has lost himself. This strengthens the 'glue' which sticks us to the travelling trio of hobbits as they enter the land of further vacuums, Mordor.

To save his protagonist from becoming too repetitively two dimensional in his responses, as we've said, Tolkien then has Frodo stung and later maimed with the loss of a finger - all drawing attention from readers with vacuum power.

Only at the end of the quest does Frodo regain whatever little personality he had at the beginning:

> Then as he had kept watch Sam had noticed that at times a light seemed to be shining faintly within; but now the light was even clearer and stronger. Frodo's face was peaceful, the marks of fear and care had left it; but it looked old, old and beautiful, as if the chiseling of the shaping years was now revealed in many fine lines that had before been hidden, though the identity of the face was not changed.

In fact, Frodo becomes emptier and emptier until in the last part of the book, his quest over, he even rejects participation in the society around him. This isn't a 'bad' thing - this is just him acting out his role as a protagonist: *a virtual walking vacuum.*

As we have seen, what normal terminology calls a 'protagonist' is actually an increasing 'black hole' of vacuum power, at least until some point in the story - towards the end - when fortunes change and vacuums get filled - or not, depending on the author's intention. If the character vacuums are filled, we're reading a Comedy or an Epic; if they are left empty, we're reading a Tragedy or an Irony.

With Pip, from the Ironic *Great Expectations*, vacuum power increases from the first page and isn't unambiguously filled on the last; Elizabeth Bennett, from the Comedy/Romance *Pride and Prejudice,* has losses that grow in significance until the turning point of the story when they begin to be fulfilled; Jane Austen's Emma in the novel that bears her name seems content at first but her character vacuum is her ignorance of her own failings. She plunges from one embarrassing mistake to the next until, in telling the tediously garrulous Miss Bates to shut up, her whole life empties.

Hamlet loses his father, his mother (to a false marriage), his girlfriend, his kingdom and, arguably, himself. His attraction as a protagonist is created by all this vacuum power.

In Henry Fielding's Epic novel *Tom Jones*, Tom is a foundling, discovered on a doorstep, makes his way through loss after loss and only at the end turns out to be well-born, and marries the girl of his dreams; Michael Henchard in the Ironic *The Mayor of Casterbridge* by Thomas Hardy is the most tragic tale of a man who does a great wrong (he sells his wife and daughter) and pays for it later. His life is ruined by Fate - and laid open to vacuums; Charlotte Brontë's heroine in the Romance *Jane Eyre* is completely admirable and compelling but over the top of such loss and emptiness that the reader almost comes to believe in supernatural intervention so that at the end of the story she can be fulfilled.

Based on this survey of a wide variety of texts - and I am sure that you can think of many more - we can safely conclude for the moment that what has been so far called a 'protagonist' is actually *the point in a story which most attracts the reader's attention with vacuums.*

Dress that character with minimal verisimilitude - fail to describe him or her, give them only a skimpy history, sketch in only a pale outline of a person - *but make sure that you take plenty away from him or her from the start, and continue to do so throughout the story.*

What are you trying to do with this odd-sounding tactical move? What is the purpose of all these vacuums?

The object of pumping characters full of more and more vacuums is *to strengthen the flow of reader attention until it becomes strong enough to prompt emotional commitment*. Given enough of that commitment, a reader will be further prompted into the physical action of turning page after page to find out how this central character vacuum, which has grabbed and held so much reader attention, will eventually be filled.

We say we 'love' our heroes - we're actually just stuck to their vacuums.

In Comedies, the vacuum is usually filled through marriage (see Elizabeth Bennett, Emma, Tom Jones and Jane Eyre above); it becomes obvious in the course of the play or novel or film that the protagonist is literally 'incomplete' without a partner.

In Epics, the hero has normally become so much of a walking vacuum that his lack can only be filled through transcending the world of the story in some way. Frodo has to leave Middle Earth and journey to the Blessed Lands; Luke Skywalker has to become a Jedi; Harry Potter has to mature into a fully-fledged wizard. Many child protagonists have to simply grow into adults. In all cases, they have to be transformed into something totally different from what they were *in order to make the point that their 'wounds' are now healed.*

In Tragedies, the vacuum is usually not filled, or filled too late or imperfectly - that's why it's a Tragedy; in Ironies, the vacuum opens out to be overwhelmingly bigger at the end, and the hero is often lost in it altogether - that's why it's an Irony. Examples include Hamlet, Macbeth, and Micheal Henchard above.

Whichever category the story falls under, the mechanical principle is the same:

There has to be enough focused vacuum power to get the reader committed, to glue the reader, to bring the reader and the writer's message together.

It's not only the protagonist that this applies to. It applies to everything in a story. In terms of the things we have been used to calling 'characters', *every single one of the templated figures from the patterns given above are also created using vacuum power.*

Here's another interesting thing: if you don't particularly have to worry about verisimilitude when you're designing your protagonist, you have to worry about it even less when you're constructing all the other things that we have formerly called 'characters'. What you are actually using are *templated archetypes,* almost like the figures in a Tarot card set.

The Comic Companion

Take the ever-present 'comic companion', mentioned earlier. He or she is virtually the same figure from tale to tale.

Sam in *The Lord of the Rings,* has remarkable similarities to Dill in *To Kill a Mockingbird,* or Piglet in *Winnie the Pooh,* or Herbert in *Great Expectations,* or Ron in *Harry Potter And The Philosopher's Stone,* or R2-D2 and C-Threepio in *Star Wars,* or the porter in *Macbeth.* Why are these figures there? Why are they so alike?

One standard answer is 'to provide comic relief'. But the real answer, the universal answer, is *to fill a minor vacuum.*

What does that mean? If the protagonist is all about being a vacuum - an ever-increasing vacuum, progressively being robbed of more and more, physically, emotionally and even spiritually, in order to draw in the reader's attention relentlessly - then a comic character provides interludes when a relatively unimportant vacuum is filled. This acts to break up the flow a little, to relieve the relentless build-up of emptiness. A side vacuum, not essential to the overall plot, is temporarily filled, bringing with it that well-known symptom of vacuum-filling: laughter. The reader, drained by the trials of the protagonist who is losing more and more as the story goes on, experiences a moment of relief. That moment of relief serves to make the protagonist's vacuums stronger by contrast.

'Comic relief' is *'vacuum relief'.*

The comic figure also has something essential to do in the end: they have a key role to play in the protagonist's quest.

Don't take my word for it - look at these examples.

In Chapter Two of *The Lord of the Rings,* Frodo has just learned how the entire fate of Middle Earth has fallen upon his shoulders and that he will have to give up everything that he loves - home, friends, comfort. Who is cutting the grass outside his window as he learns this in a deep conversation with the wizard Gandalf? Sam, who is comically lifted through the window by the wizard and comically regards the whole prospect of the trip as a blessing.

Sam later plays a key role in the quest to destroy the Ring.

After an onslaught into her childhood from the adult world, with racism explicitly appearing, Scout is confronted by the word 'rape' and the threatened loss of her friendship with her brother Jem. Who should reappear at that moment in the novel *To Kill a Mockingbird* but Dill, the comic figure, who comforts Scout that night.

Dill is the one who prompts the children to seek out Boo Radley earlier in the novel, which has huge consequences later.

After the great ordeal towards the end of the novel in which Pip finds out the awful truth about his benefactor and then loses him, who steps forward to fill Pip's vacuum with some comfort but Herbert, the comic figure in *Great Expectations*.

Herbert then provides Pip with support at a vital moment in the plot.

As for *Star Wars*, comic companions R2-D2 and C-Threepio are constantly acting as vacuum-fillers in their appearances after or during major battle scenes. They act to rescue the heroes at crucial moments. And the porter in *Macbeth* appears with his word-play and lewd jokes just after Macbeth's horrific treasonous murder of Duncan, as a result of which Macbeth believes he has lost his own soul. (It's also the porter who symbolically lets in Macduff, the character who will bring an end to Macbeth's reign.)

In all these cases, we have yawning abysses of our protagonists - active, expanding vacuums, serving their real purpose of sucking at the reader's attention, drawing out commitment like a vampire drawing blood - and the momentary relief of a templated comic figure, who is less affected by the mounting vacuum and who fills a minor vacuum unexpectedly, prompting the response which we have come to know as 'comic relief' but which is actually mechanically better described as *a temporary filling of vacuums*.

The Female Companion

What about the romantic partner figure - in Epics and Tragedies often a woman, in Ironies and Comedies, sometimes a man? Are they also some kind of templated 'type'? What do they have to do with vacuums?

A Passage to India, by E.M. Forster, is a masterpiece of a novel in which the vacuums run out of control, as they tend to do in Ironies. The resulting emptiness is best symbolised in the book by the Marabar Caves, which contain nothing but a sense of meaninglessness.

> Nothing is inside them, they were sealed up before the creation of pestilence or treasure; if mankind grew curious and excavated, nothing, nothing would be added to the sum of good or evil. One of them is rumoured within the boulder that swings on the summit of the highest of the hills; a bubble-shaped cave that has neither ceiling nor floor, and mirrors its own darkness in every direction infinitely. If the boulder falls and smashes, the cave will smash too – empty as an Easter egg.

The caves grip the imagination of the female characters Adela and Mrs. Moore, effectively driving Mrs. Moore to her death and Adela temporarily insane. Neither finds peace or wholeness again - Adela returns to England shattered by her experience, unable to marry the man she went to India for. Because it's an Irony, in *A Passage to India* the vacuums win and the female figure is left empty, tormented (Adela suffers physical agonies, Mrs. Moore mental ones) and unsatisfied.

Pride and Prejudice, by Jane Austen, on the other hand, is a prototype of the romantic novel and so fits in the Comedy quarter of our Wheel of Fiction. Here, Lizzy, potentially a tragic figure, ends up overcoming her vacuum and is fulfilled, marrying Darcy at the end.

Jane in *Jane Eyre*, on the other hand, walks around the novel much like a living vacuum for most of the story, but there's a deeper female vacuum lurking upstairs in the mad wife, and (though it almost sounds like a lewd joke) Jane's vacuum is eventually filled by Rochester.

Cathy in *Wuthering Heights*, ends up unwell, dead and then a ghost - haunting the moors like a phantom vacuum.

In *Macbeth*, Lady Macbeth ends up walking, empty of soul, in her sleep and then committing suicide; in *Hamlet*, Ophelia loses her mind and also throws her own life away; in *Great Expectations*, Miss Havisham is a hollow ghost and Estella an emotionless shell.

Are you beginning to see a pattern here?

Put aside the idea that a character in a work of fiction is a creature designed to reflect reality in terms of appearing lifelike and 'real' to readers, and instead think of what you call characters as *constructions made of vacuums*.

Accepting that then empowers you to further see this pattern:

Female figures in fiction are often personified vacuums.

In Comedies and Epics, these personifications are matched with a corresponding vacuum-filler and the character is either married or matched up in a satisfying way; in Tragedies and Ironies, their personification becomes more intense, resulting in suicides, hauntings, madness, prolonged emptiness and other kinds of living death.

A Winter Comedy like *It's a Wonderful Life*, containing as it does a tale-within-a-tale, or an Irony within a Comedy, shows us both extremes: in the Ironic sub-tale, Mary is a barren spinster doomed to work alone in a library; in the enclosing Comedy, she is completely fulfilled by marriage to George whom she has hungered for all her life.

A Winter Epic like *Alien*, possessed of dark overtones but basically following an Epic template, has its female protagonist threatened with rape by a robot and consumption by a monster before allowing her to escape either at the last minute. Ironically and in keeping with the Ironic mood, the hungry vacuum-driven alien is cancelled out at last by the larger vacuum of space.

The Black Widow in the Winter Epic *Captain America: The Winter Soldier* is composed almost completely of vacuums: mysteries, unresolved backstory clues, hints of betrayal, a good example of personified vacuums.

Forget about characters as living, breathing people: start thinking of them as *constructs* built with the raw material of *emptinesses*. It's almost the other way around from what we have been brought up to think: the resulting figure in a story resembles a boy or a girl, a man or a woman, but is actually the outward manifestation of a *composite of vacuums*.

Nothing of this has any real connection to 'real life' or masculine or feminine genders necessarily. We are talking about *fictional constructs*.

The Warrior Figure

Obvious as Aragorn in *The Lord of the Rings*, or Hans Solo in *Star Wars*, less obvious as Fielding in *A Passage to India* or Sirius Black in *Harry Potter*, the warrior figure has some common traits too across the world of fiction. Warrior figures tend to start off as duplicitous - they are presented to the reader as potentially villainous, not quite to be trusted, shadowy. This ambiguity is their characteristic quality. That uncertainty about them is of course a vacuum, a gap, an unknown.

In Comedies and Epics they often emerge as the love interests for the female figures - examples abound, including Darcy and Captain Wentworth in Austen's novels, who begin somewhat overshadowed but who are redeemed by their heroines later.

In Tragedies and Ironies, these warrior types are often the 'heroic' counterparts to the anti-heroic protagonists: Laertes to Hamlet, Malcolm to Macbeth, Boo Radley to Bob Ewell in *To Kill a Mockingbird*, Samuel L. Jackson's Jules Winnfield to John Travolta's Vincent Vega in *Pulp Fiction*.

They eventually shake off the suggestions of duality, though. Their vacuums are filled and they become kings, generals or leaders, doers, men of action and command. It is Aragorn who wins the military side of the War of the Ring, Hans Solo who rescues Luke and goes on to become a general, Fielding who stands up against British injustice in the trial of Adela, Sirius Black who commands power in Harry Potter. Darcy loses his pride and becomes a mover of events; Boo Radley comes out of hiding to save the children; Jules Winnfield rejects his criminal background and decides to 'walk the earth'.

So these characters we have become accustomed to call warrior figures are figures in transition and move out of their vacuums in the course of a wide variety of fiction.

It must be becoming pretty obvious to even the most sceptical reader that characters are constructs, and that all fiction uses the same types of constructs. They are made out of vacuums, because vacuums *move* things.

What do they move?

In fiction, vacuums move reader attention.

What we have been used to calling 'character motivation' can be better expressed as simple vacuum power. All these figures are moved by vacuums: the protagonist by his or her inner or outer wounds, scars or losses; the comic companions balance this with an injection of vacuum-filler; the female figures personify vacuums; the warrior figures emerge from their vacuums.

The whole world of 'character-driven fiction' is here: reader attention pulled along by vacuums within archetypal figures.

The Strange Case of The Old Man with the Stick

What about 'plot-driven fiction'? Well, there's still one major figure who we touched upon earlier: the old man with a stick.

He opens the door to the central plot vacuum.

What else do these figures have in common?

The old-man-with-a-stick figure ranges from Gandalf in *The Lord of the Rings*, Dumbledore in *Harry Potter*, Obi Wan Kenobi in *Star Wars*, the Doctor in *Doctor Who,* and so on right the way through to their Tragic, Ironic or Comedic reflections, like Jaggers in *Great Expectations*, Jacob Marley in *A Christmas Carol*, Clarence in *It's a Wonderful Life*, or Doc Smith in *Back to the Future*.

All of them play the role of *establishing the major plot vacuum for the tale of which they are a part.*

Gandalf reveals the history of the One Ring which sets the story in motion; Dumbledore outlines the tasks that Harry must accomplish; Obi Wan sets out the nature of the quest for Luke and his companions; the Doctor always sees the way through to the conclusion of each episode's plot. Jaggers in *Great Expectations* lays out the law, literally, which moves Pip forward; Jacob Marley in *A Christmas Carol*, outlines the challenge faced by Scrooge; Clarence in *It's a Wonderful Life* is the force behind the main plot element of that film; Doc Smith in *Back to the Future similarly* drives the story into action plot-wise. They are the main expositors; we turn to them for an idea of what the plot is going to be about.

Then all of them, across the vast range of stories under consideration here, disappear. They usually die, vanishing from the story for at least a while. Then they all return, even from beyond death.

Why is that?

They disappear largely because their function in the story is completed. Even in the child's tale *The Hobbit*, Gandalf disappears for a large portion of the adventure because the plot vacuum is so well established at that point that there is no need for him. He only returns when there is a requirement for further 'vacuum clarification' during the Battle of the Five Armies. Even Badger in *The Wind in the Willows* plays no real part in the tale until he has to set the plot goal for the last part of the book, the recapture of Toad Hall.

In *A Midsummer Night's Dream*, the old man Egeus, having laid the ground rules for the unfolding of the story, exits the stage until right at the end; once Nick Fury has laid out the role of the superheroes in *The Avengers*, he takes a back seat.

Jaggers in *Great Expectations* presents the groundwork of the plot and (because *Great Expectations* is an Irony) conceals its implications; Clarence in *It's a Wonderful Life*, or Doc Smith in *Back to the Future* both mechanically make the entire plot happen by generating the big plot vacuum themselves. In *To Kill a Mockingbird*, Atticus sets out the parameters of what the story is all about but takes a minimal role for many chapters, disappearing from the story for large sections.

That type of fiction familiar to us as 'plot-driven' turns out to be a set-up - a set-up organised and masterminded by the character figure known as the old man with a stick.

All these character figures turn out to be almost as identical as mathematical functions.

And they are all in the thing called a story to serve particular purposes.

You'll see why all this works technically shortly.

Summary

So characters possess vacuums of one kind or another. These are *character vacuums*. They are essential in any story that you want to connect to a reader. The old man figure is the one who bridges over into the *plot vacuums*, which come in various kinds, as we shall see next.

Can the characters in your own fiction be redesigned so that they are composed of needs, emptinesses, missing things? Already, just in thinking about these modifications, you will be bringing your story to life.

Turn the things called 'characters' into vacuum constructs.

Paradoxically, by almost mechanically treating them that way, they come to life for the reader.

Connect them all up in some way and you will have established a working channel for your message. You will have set up a means of getting through to the reader. Leave out the vacuums, design your characters to be 'as close as possible to real life', and your story will remain unread by anyone except you - and even you will know that there's something wrong with it. You need to prompt your reader, guide or move him or her, stir and arouse the vacuum within the reader, make that inner vacuum more real and give it a little jolt or push.

The same applies to the thing called 'plot'.

Chapter Six:
Plot Vacuums

If the things that we have become accustomed to calling 'characters' are actually vacuums disguised as people, then we have the answer to all character-driven fiction: what drives the fiction isn't actually 'character' at all, it's *vacuums*.

Plots are the same. Are they driven by emotion? Action? Drama? Conflict? These things are all indications that what is actually driving the story is *vacuums*.

You'll read a lot in other guides or tomes full of advice to do with fiction about using emotion to engage your potential reader. Aristotle called this use of emotion 'pathos'. It's powerful and common.

But what creates these emotions? Vacuums.

Vacuums are reliable; vacuums are dependable. Plus they are quite mechanical in nature. Their existence explains why 'popular' literature sells so well even when it's not particularly 'well written'. The almost physical force which a cleverly crafted vacuum can deploy is what compels emotional commitment by readers.

A strong vacuum attracts emotional commitment.

What you are aiming for with characters and plots is to generate vacuums so powerful that they drag the reader through any obstacle on the way to your message.

How do you do that?

By making them larger.

We've touched on the many levels of vacuum from basic to universal. Successful fiction shows the reader through the medium of the story what would happen if a vacuum grew worse or wider or larger or more intense or whatever is applicable. What if the loss of an innocuous luxury tapped into a deeper loss of companionship and then that led to a threat to life itself? The reader, imagining this, moves towards greater need and gets closer to acquiring your meaningful message.

There is a moment in successful fiction when a reader becomes completely committed to the work. Perhaps they are tracking with a character figure who is in emotional pain and needs a remedy, as in *Great Expectations*; perhaps they are attracted by the vacuums of a scene in which there is an urgent need for an item to defuse an imminent explosion, as in the film thriller *Juggernaut*; perhaps they are glued to a chase scene as in the films *Speed* or *The French Connection* or the children's book *The Lion, the Witch and the Wardrobe*. In the case of the committed reader, they need something and they are going to get it, regardless, even if it means reading all night.

How did they get to that point?

Readers, like the character figure to whom you have 'stuck' them with character vacuums, are prompted to action by plot vacuums in the story. As they are driven further forward by plot vacuums, they become urgently aware of the greater need that is developing and are in full motion towards it. They just want to get to the climax of the story, the vacuum-filling moment.

Fiction writing is the process of creating or boosting vacuums until motion is achieved towards the fulfilling ending.

Successful fiction writers simply work with vacuums until the reader overcomes his or her own inertia and makes that commitment, as per the following diagram.

If your message fills the vacuum accurately, fulfilment is obtained, trust is achieved and the reader will return to your writing in the future to have vacuums filled again. Thus great literature is born.

But how do we get to the point where the vacuum is so strong that all reader inertia is overcome?

We'll start with a simple case study, a contemporary movie, to give you a sense of how this works, then get more technical later so that you will see *why* it works. When you fully grasp the how and the why, you will be in complete command of your readers forever.

Protagonist (and therefore reader) ready to have vacuums filled

Protagonist (and therefore reader) prompted to move forward by plot vacuums

Old man with a stick 'attention commander' figure impinges upon awareness of protagonist

PROTAGONIST URGENTLY AWARE OF GREATEST NEED (BASIC VACUUM)

PROTAGONIST INCREASINGLY AWARE OF GREATER NEED

PROTAGONIST EXPERIENCES A UNIVERSAL VACUUM, BUT IS UNAWARE OF DEEPER NEED

At this point, you should try and dispense with any previous knowledge or training in this area as what you're about to learn here is too simple - and too powerful - for any of that. You may find many reasons why this is 'too simple' and 'needs to be more complex'. It doesn't.

The Four Kinds of Plot Vacuum

There are four kinds of plot vacuum:

Linear vacuums - best summed up by the question 'What happens next?'

Mystery vacuums - encapsulated by the question 'What's really going on?'

Moral vacuums - as in the question 'What is the right thing in this situation?'

and

Core vacuums - summed up as what the story is really all about.

Core vacuums are entangled with answers to the biggest questions, 'What are the big problems we're trying to solve?' 'What is the message or solution we're trying to communicate?' and 'What is the goal which we're trying to attract others to?'

Core vacuums in stories equate to *basic vacuums*: risks to basics like life, health, personal well-being and so on. They are the engines, the 'nuclear reactors' of fiction.

Mystery vacuums ask questions like 'What's really going on?' 'What is happening under the surface?' and 'What unknown needs to be known?' We don't know, and we want to know - and that *want* is a vacuum.

Mystery vacuums stick us to the story at every possible point. They are the 'glue' of fiction.

Linear vacuums ask simple questions like 'What happens next?' or 'What unknown comes next?' Simpler than a mystery vacuum, they are part of the woof and warp of even the most primitive stories.

Linear vacuums drive us forward. They create the *momentum* of fiction.

Moral vacuums ask the questions 'What's right and wrong here?' 'What about consequences?' and 'What should be done?' We are in a quandary - and that *uncertainty* is a vacuum.

Moral vacuums engage our innermost selves. They help to create the *meaning* of fiction.

'Captain America: The Winter Soldier'

To understand what these things are and how they work together to produce a story, let's take the example of the film *Captain America: The Winter Soldier*. This is a classic Winter Epic in form, following the template as described earlier almost perfectly, and close scrutiny shows that it also makes expert use of all the above kinds of plot vacuum, knowingly or not.

Of course, a well-known Marvel Comics character like Captain America has a fan-following numbering in millions anyway. Furthermore, any Marvel fan has already been hooked into watching this film by the phenomenal success of the Marvel cinematic universe, in particular the film *The Avengers*, one of the top-grossing films of all time. So we already have the fan who will camp outside the theatre on opening night to see the film first; and we already have an interested public, not quite as desperate but nevertheless gripped by the ongoing saga that unfolds throughout the Marvel films.

What about those potential audience members who know nothing about Captain America at all? How are they attracted?

Before the film starts, we already have some character vacuums: the back story of Steve Rogers, the eponymous hero of the story, who has not only lost his parents by this film, but his whole time period, 1940s America. He's survived being frozen and has awakened to a whole new world as shown in the comics and in the initial film in the series, *Captain America, the First Avenger*. For audiences less familiar with this character vacuum, we see it triggered by observing in the opening scenes Rogers not understanding basic modern concepts like the internet when making friends with Sam Wilson. Rogers becomes the protagonist for all the audience precisely because he is *the constructed figure in the story who attracts most of the reader's attention with character vacuums.*

The story is set up to be driven by these character vacuums. Based on this, we should expect that towards the end of the film, Rogers will 'rediscover himself' - in other words, he will have that vacuum filled, at least partially. And that is what we do find.

But how are the plot vacuums constructed?

The initial and most basic plot vacuum is the one which drives even the most primitive fiction, drawn from the simple question:

'What happens next?'

This is a *linear vacuum*. It is the emptiness created as soon as anyone starts writing a story based on sequence - which is just about any story: what is the next occurrence in a chain of occurrences? The gap or missing answer to that question draws the reader on.

Where the expertise comes in is in constructing a linear vacuum *which the reader cares about filling*. Thus, we see the character vacuum established first, as described above, in the opening scene. Then, in the action sequence set on board a ship at the beginning of the film, it is the fast-paced placing of one linear vacuum after another which draws the viewer along: who will win the next hand-to-hand combat? How will the apparently overwhelming odds be overcome? How will Rogers defeat Batroc without his shield? and so on. It wouldn't work as well if we didn't already care about the Rogers character as the prime vacuum-surrounded figure.

These linear vacuums are typical of all action films or stories based on simplistic action. We are accustomed by certain conventions that come as part of the Epic package that the hero will beat up the bad guys, though the scene's power comes from the vacuum of not knowing exactly how that will happen when the bad guys seem to have the upper hand.

Linear vacuums draw power not only from the unspoken question 'What will happen next?' but also from its associated question 'How will it happen?'. A linear vacuum is boosted whenever the odds are stacked against the protagonist - which occurs in almost every story, as you may have noticed in your own reading or viewing. The reason that these odds are increased is usually given as 'it escalates the drama or tension'. What is actually happening is that having the protagonist face greater and greater barriers acts to *magnify the vacuum in the reader's or viewer's mind* generated by the question 'What will happen next?' and *this* is what draws the reader or viewer on.

Fights, chases, hunts, quests: these are all typical forms of linear vacuums.

Linear vacuums give the story *momentum*.

But linear vacuums alone are often not enough. What spices things up or takes things to the next level is the next category of plot vacuum, the *mystery vacuum* based on the question:

'What is really going on?'

It is the additional, unexpected vacuum of not knowing exactly what Natasha Romanoff, the Black Widow, is doing in these early scenes of the film that sets up the mystery.

Romanoff, by hacking into the enemies' computer and downloading data, seems to be doing something contrary to what Rogers is doing, and of which Rogers is unaware. This is a mystery vacuum: in this case, unknown intentions in a character leading to a mystery which sucks in our attention even more. Rogers discovers Romanoff has another agenda: to extract data from the ship's computers for Nick Fury, Rogers' boss and the director of S.H.I.E.L.D., the agency which employs him. The resolution of the 'What happens next?' - good guy beating bad guy in physical combat - is underpinned quickly by this unexpected mystery.

That underlying mystery vacuum is what carries us forward into the next scene when Rogers returns to the Triskelion, S.H.I.E.L.D.'s headquarters. He confronts Fury who is not forthcoming, which prolongs and deepens the mystery vacuum. Rogers is then briefed about Project Insight: three Heli-carriers, giant airborne destroyers, linked to spy satellites, designed to preemptively eliminate threats.

While these are impressive visually and as a threat, they don't fill the mystery vacuum that has been established but only serve to amplify it. This is an example of 'vacuum interconnection': what are all these heli-carriers for? Their presence taps into *common* and *basic* vacuums - personal freedom, life and death - and so raises the stakes and the vacuum power in the story.

It's no accident that it's Nick Fury who gives Rogers this briefing: Fury is after all the 'old man with a stick' in this story. It's his function to outline the deeper vacuums of the tale, as described earlier. It's also here that we glimpse our first *moral vacuum*: Rogers questions whether Project Insight is the right thing to do. As an audience, our own morality is engaged and the story gains meaning.

The reason why we begin to care is the character vacuums and the sense of unresolved mystery around Fury's actions. Older guides to fiction might have called this 'conflict' and claimed that it had to be present in any story - what it actually is is the operation of *mystery vacuums*, sucking in attention from the audience and channelling it more or less wherever the screenplay writer wishes, if he or she understands vacuum power.

Fury himself then develops his own character vacuum, set up in his dialogue in the elevator with Rogers, suggesting a lack of trust in others from a past in which he has lost much. Note that he already has a trademark character vacuum symbol, the wound or scar - his missing eye. That he then reveals that he doesn't know what is on the encrypted drive recovered by Romanoff connects him to the mystery vacuum too.

Our attention is therefore literally glued to Fury as we move into the next scene. His inability to decrypt the data recovered by Romanoff magnifies the mystery vacuum even more. Fury becomes suspicious about Project Insight and asks senior S.H.I.E.L.D. official Alexander Pierce (Robert Redford) to delay the project while he tries to find out more. The film's audience is also tracking with the desire to find out more and are thus becoming allied to the construct we know as the 'character' Fury.

This is what makes the next scene so powerful. On his way to rendezvous with agent Maria Hill, Fury is ambushed by whole squad of assailants led by the mysterious assassin (another mystery vacuum) called the Winter Soldier. Our sympathies now lie with the Fury figure in his quest to solve the mystery. But something else comes into play here too, as outlined above.

The odds stacked against the character magnify the size of the vacuum.

This leads to one of the key formulas of vacuum power: the more antagonists there are, the more powerful they seem, and the more apparent force used against the protagonist, the greater the vacuum power.

It also leads to an important fundamental question: if a protagonist is redefined as the central point of vacuum generation, what is an antagonist?

An antagonist is almost a by-product of the necessity for vacuum power around any protagonist. Antagonists are usually defined as the opposites of protagonists, the figures with whom the protagonist struggles.

But again, why? Why do almost all stories feature this figure (with remarkable similarities across the boards, as we will see)?

If, as we say, a protagonist is defined as the main point of vacuum generation within a story, then, by deduction, the antagonist must be some kind of anti-vacuum. He or she, if we are correct, should be found trying to deny vacuums all over the place; he or she should be obsessed with enforcing some kind of solution on all concerned.

And that is in fact what we find.

Antagonists

Antagonists come with answers and messages of their own; they are the opposite to the protagonist.

This goes right back to the intention of the author: if an author wants to create a Comedy or an Epic - in other words, a story with a positive ending - the antagonist of that story will be creating sorrow and negativity; if an author wants to relate a victory, an antagonist will be trying to bring about defeat. In Comedies and Epics, antagonists answer the moral vacuum the *wrong* way.

If an author wants to create a Tragedy or an Irony - a story with a negative ending - then the 'antagonist' of that tale will be the one trying to bring joy or positivity. If the author is focused on defeat, this character will be aiming for victory. In Tragedies and Ironies, this character tries to answer the moral vacuum the *right* way - but the world is against him or her.

Where the protagonist of a tale is full of growing vacuums, the antagonist will have ever-mounting solutions. In Comedies and Epics, these solutions are enforced, unwanted, false; in Tragedies and Ironies they are weak, misguided or doomed.

The antagonist's purpose is hinted at in the early part of a tale, then grows in proportion to the vacuum power. As we will see, there are surprisingly similar patterns in all of this.

Antagonists in stories are all almost identical: they are all compulsively trying to wipe out all kinds of vacuums by force, and imperfectly, with their own messages, or some kind of projection of themselves.

They command great power in Comedies and Epics, having many allies and usually overwhelming force or the suggestion of it, but they end up defeated. In Tragedies and Ironies they are likewise often overpowering - but triumphant.

Examples abound: Sauron in *The Lord of the Rings*; Voldemort in *Harry Potter*; Chancellor Palpatine in the *Star Wars* series; the witches in *Macbeth*; the White Witch in *The Lion, the Witch and the Wardrobe*; Morgana le Fey in the Arthur legends; and so on. All either have conquered the world or threaten to take it over, or at least to dominate the local area of the story; all come with an antipathetic message; all seem to possess some kind of overwhelming power. And they have other things in common too, as we shall see.

One of them is this: there is usually a close connection between the character construct we call the protagonist and the character construct we call the antagonist. Think of Luke Skywalker and his father Darth Vader; think of Frodo and the supernatural link with Sauron through the Ring; think of Harry Potter and the scar that connects him with Voldemort. Even in other genres, this connection is stark: *Pride and Prejudice*'s Darcy is antagonist Lady Catherine du Bergh's relative, for example. The connection can be symbolic rather than familial or 'magical', but it seems to be always there - even Bob Ewell in *To Kill a Mockingbird* is a quasi-father compared with Atticus's real father figure.

We could leave it there, having established that there is usually this connection, odd though it may seem. But, in common with the rest of this book, the question is Why? And it has an answer: if the antagonist's job is to try to destroy all vacuums by force, with twisted, imperfect 'solutions', then the most intimate vacuum they must try and fill will be the central character vacuum of the story - i.e., the inner need of the protagonist. If we look, that's exactly what we find: Vader, Sauron, Voldemort, Lady Catherine du Bergh, Miss Havisham, Bob Ewell, *Macbeth's* witches, and all the rest all make the effort throughout their stories to fill the mind of the protagonist with lies and false solutions, ranging from the Dark Side of the Force to racist prejudice and sinister prophecy.

In effect, the antagonist is another kind of shadow for the protagonist, but one who more nearly succeeds in overcoming him or her. Where the protagonist is saved and the connection severed, we have Epics or Comedies; where the protagonist is overwhelmed, we have Tragedies and Ironies.

We'll return to antagonists later. In *Captain America: The Winter Soldier*, the antagonist is Pierce and the shadow protagonist is the Winter Soldier - his connection with the protagonist is that he used to be the hero's sidekick, and he's the only living remnant of Steve Rogers' lost 1940s world.

Core Vacuums in 'Captain America: The Winter Soldier'

Continuing with our analysis of the film, after escaping the Winter Soldier, a wounded Fury escapes to Rogers' apartment, and completes his 'old man with a stick' role by outlining the story's core vacuum, the Big Story, warning him that S.H.I.E.L.D. is compromised. After handing Rogers a flash drive containing data from the ship, Fury is gunned down by the Winter Soldier, who then escapes. Fury then dies in surgery. (Fury fulfils his role as the 'old man with a stick' archetype here too, and so we suspect that he might be back later in the story. The 'stick' in this case is literally the USB stick with all the revelatory data on it.) This further intensifies the vacuum power for the audience: not only has Fury apparently been slain with all the potential knowledge he could have cast upon the situation, but Rogers and Romanoff now have further character vacuums, both losing a respected mentor figure.

Rogers' *universal* vacuum - the inconvenience of not really grasping the society around him - has been magnified into a *common* vacuum: the real loss of a close friend and ally.

Thus another key datum becomes apparent:

The apparent death of the old man with a stick mentor figure is a classic method of giving the protagonist a more powerful dose of vacuum power.

This figure dies in almost all classic Epic fiction, with the same effect on the protagonist, Consider these obvious examples: Gandalf/Frodo; Obi Wan Kenobi/Luke Skywalker; Dumbledore/Harry Potter. Less obvious examples abound and will be considered later.

As you can see, the screenplay writers have really done nothing else than create various kinds of vacuums and work to make them larger. These are then amplified further as the story proceeds. This isn't an aimless progression - it's heading somewhere specific, as we are about to see.

Pierce summons Rogers to the Triskelion and when Rogers withholds Fury's information, Pierce brands him a fugitive. Both Rogers and female companion archetype Romanoff are then ruthlessly pursued and hunted by the antagonists, in a classic linear vacuum hunt. Old methods of story analysis might have called this 'increasing the tension' or 'delineating the conflict between the protagonists and the antagonists' but what is at work behind it is vacuums. It's not so much a battle between protagonist and antagonist as it is a playing out of vacuum power which drives the story forward: the audience is glued to the screen by the question how will these vacuums, plot and character alike, get filled? The linear vacuums created by 'What happens next?' combine with the mystery vacuums generated by 'What is really going on?' which add to the character vacuums to build a vacuum-powered machine.

This all leads up to the impressive antagonist's apparent triumph in the next section of the film: villain Arnim Zola reveals to Rogers and

Romanoff that ever since S.H.I.E.L.D. was founded after World War II, Nazi offshoot Hydra has secretly operated within its ranks, sowing global chaos with the long-term aim that humanity would willingly surrender its freedom in exchange for security. Now the game plan is laid out and that initial mystery vacuum of the encrypted data resolved. Now we are in *basic vacuum* territory: loss or threat to security and life itself. The vacuum power initialised in the opening action sequence has been focused, magnified and intensified into a *core vacuum*, with one sole aim, whether the screenplay writers knew about vacuum power or not:

To get audience commitment to the rest of the story.

What happens between readers and stories has been called many things in the past, including the 'willing suspension of disbelief', but it is every fiction writer's first aim: to engage the reader (or in the case of a film, the viewer) to such a degree that they will 'go with' the rest of the story. They are committed to it; they have emotionally invested in it.

Now as an audience we are subject to a classic core vacuum: the stakes are raised, and Hydra is about the reveal itself to the world and place millions of lives and the vital freedoms of society at risk. This is where the question is no longer 'What happens next?' as much as 'How can the antagonist be stopped?' Basic and common vacuums - the desire for life and for freedom and safety - have all been tapped into. Rogers explicitly fills the moral vacuum with a decision to fight for freedom, no matter what. Now it is the role of the core vacuum to take things to the highest possible 'notch', to involve the maximum possible pulling power.

It's a point which is usually aligned with the naming or outing or otherwise revealing the story's real antagonist. Rogers and Romanoff realise what the audience have probably seen at least since Pearce named Rogers as a fugitive: that their enemy has been Pearce as a Hydra leader all along. There's no point in keeping that mysterious any longer - to some degree, mystery vacuums have been superseded by the core vacuum which will carry the viewer through to the end of the tale.

So what we are accustomed to describing as the 'plot' has so far been a string of different types of vacuums leading up to a point of commitment and to the core vacuum.

What Happens if Vacuum Power is Reduced?

What would have happened had linear, mystery and moral vacuums *not* been used to attract and glue viewers to the screen in various ways? Could the story have worked without them? Would the audience have accepted the 'Hydra threatens the world' scenario without the prior build-up?

The honest answer is yes, they probably would - but the film would have far less emotional power and the audience would have invested very little in the outcome. Character vacuums, linear vacuums, mystery vacuums and moral vacuums have all helped produce an emotional commitment to the story where the viewers care far more about the final result than they otherwise would have.

That's the difference between a shallow 'good versus evil' tale which tries to jump straight into the core vacuum, and a story which acquires the participation of the audience or reader using character, linear, mystery and moral vacuums. Lesser or simpler stories are built around a core vacuum and nothing else - they depend on voluntary reader/viewer participation, if you like. More complex and more successful stories use every vacuum at their disposal to almost compel reader or viewer commitment.

In an Epic like *Captain America: The Winter Soldier*, the rest of the tale is now a matter of the protagonist working towards filling the story's core vacuum, whatever the odds and however unlikely the events which follow. Somehow, Steve Rogers has to defeat the enemy and prevent basic vacuums created by threats to life and freedom from growing out of control - he has to find the real vacuum filler, which is always the author's central message: Joy, or Sorrow; Victory, or Defeat.

This Marvel movie was a success at the box office and critically. It was no accident. It's a story which weaves the various types of plot vacuums - linear, moral, mystery and core - with the standard character vacuums as exemplified by Rogers, Romanoff, Fury and Wilson. Wilson plays out his role as 'comic companion' with vital assistance or vacuum-filling; Fury returns from the dead to delineate the final core vacuum; Romanoff as the female companion finds some satisfaction at the end of the film; and Rogers, who had an inner emptiness and uncertainty for the first part of the story, comes to deeper self-knowledge and certainty in the second part. The interaction between plot and character vacuums makes for a more satisfying vacuum-filling finale and denouement. Less successful fiction relies on too few of these vacuums, if they are even aware of them at all, and generally fails to connect them up in any meaningful way.

Plot Vacuums and the Four Genres

These patterns apply across the four broad genres: Epic, Tragic, Ironic and Comic.

In Tragedies, our commitment to the cause of the protagonist is largely obtained through the working of the central figure's internal character vacuum. This attracts and absorbs reader attention until we feel pity for him or her. Once that commitment is achieved, the reader or audience can feel nothing but sadness as that protagonist, irrevocably taking on the characteristics of an antagonist, works through the core vacuum to his or her inevitable demise. Examples include Shakespeare's *King Lear* and *Macbeth*, as well as the tale of Darth Vader in *Star Wars* or Severus Snape in the *Harry Potter* series.

In Ironies, the increase in vacuum power continues exponentially past the point of commitment until we as readers or viewers are caught in a hellish downward spiral leading only to a nightmare or a perpetual emptiness resembling insanity. Think of *Fight Club* or *Brazil* in film terms, or *1984* as a novel.

In Comedies and Romances, after the point of commitment is reached we can look forward to the core vacuum being filled, usually with marriage or social reconciliation. The true antagonist is revealed and expunged and all becomes well. This is obvious in *Pride and Prejudice*, for example.

Shadow Protagonists

Captain America: The Winter Soldier has some other features of interest too.

During the film, for example, Rogers recognises the Winter Soldier as Bucky Barnes, his friend who was captured and experimented upon during WWII. Barnes is the shadow protagonist, outlined earlier: as his name suggests, he is the 'Winter' soldier to Rogers' 'super' soldier. This 'shadow' figure appears in other stories in various genres: Gollum in *The Lord of the Rings*; Malfoy in Harry Potter; Anakin Skywalker in the *Star Wars* film series; Bentley Drummle and Orlick in *Great Expectations*; Wickham in *Pride and Prejudice*; and so on.

'Shadow protagonists' serve the same purpose as almost any figure in any successful work of fiction: they increase vacuum power. By painting a picture of a character similar to the protagonist but emptier and darker, the writer suggests even more losses or threats of loss. Could the protagonist become his or her darker self? Does the destiny of the hero depend on knife-edge decisions? These are linear vacuums of the 'What could happen next?' variety. They also serve to hook in readers and glue them to the page.

Summary

Fiction writers are usually of a mindset to 'have original ideas' and then to pump them out onto the page: images, ideas, 'real' characters, lots of conflict, and a three-act structure are said to be the winning ingredients, along with the 'journey' of the protagonist through a sequence of events.

These are big mistakes.

They are mistakes made by almost every writer on the planet. Following that advice on its own creates an uphill struggle and countless texts and millions of words of fiction-writing advice. Most of it is not entirely true, and is wasteful, exhausting and boring.

The answer to getting, holding and keeping readers is much simpler:

Only powerful enough vacuums will motivate the reader to overcome his or her own inertia so that he or she makes an emotional commitment to the story.

The writer should only address those things that attract the reader: needs, emptinesses, vacuums, missing things.

Talk about wounds, scars, missing parents, dangers, mysteries, risks and ever-increasing stakes and the reader will become more and more committed to the story. Plug lesser vacuums in to common vacuums about loss of companionship or education and then plug those into basic vacuums such as threats to shelter, health and life.

In other words, write about anything that makes vacuums bigger and needs greater. What about writing about ideas, images, things you want to write about? That's all very well, but if you want to attract readers, you'll need vacuums.

Chapter Seven:
'The Lion, the Witch and the Wardrobe'
- A Case Study

Let's look at another example to see how character, linear, mystery, moral and core vacuums work together to produce a successful story.

In C. S. Lewis's world-famous children's book, *The Lion, the Witch and the Wardrobe*, we begin with four children whose initial character vacuum is the same: they have lost their homes and (at least temporarily) their parents due to the Second World War, taking place 'off-stage' when the story begins. The opening sentence establishes the extent of the initial vacuum:

> Once there were four children whose names were Peter, Susan, Edmund and Lucy. This story is about something that happened to them when they were sent away from London during the war because of the air-raids.

After Lucy discovers a magical portal, our attention is hooked by a strong mystery vacuum: what is really going on with a wardrobe that leads to another world? Fantasy vacuums play on the mystery of magic: what if the world as the reader normally knows it is not all that there is?

> 'This must be a simply enormous wardrobe!' thought Lucy, going still further in and pushing the soft folds of the coats aside to make room for her. Then she noticed that there was something crunching under her feet. 'I wonder is that more mothballs?' she thought, stooping down to feel it with her hand. But instead of feeling the hard, smooth wood of the floor of the wardrobe, she felt something soft and powdery and extremely cold.

This kind of mystery vacuum carries a great deal of power if managed correctly. It underlies much of the success of the fantasy and science fiction genres and plays a large role in children's literature precisely because, for children, the 'normal' world isn't yet as totally settled as it is for most adults. The mystery vacuum is broad and taps into such questions as 'What is the true nature of reality?'

In Lewis's work, before long, character vacuums kick in: Lucy, her visit to Narnia challenged, loses the trust of her older brothers and sister. Once all the children are in Narnia, Lucy then loses her new friend Mr. Tumnus and, in an escalating series of vacuums, the children soon afterwards lose their brother Edmund.

Before long, it's clear that Edmund is more deeply lacking the empathic qualities of the others. He takes on some of the characteristics of an antagonist: a character construct who is busy filling vacuums incorrectly or falsely.

> The silence and the loneliness were dreadful. In fact I really think he might have given up the whole plan and gone back and owned up and made friends with the others, if he hadn't happened to say to himself, 'When I'm King of Narnia the first thing I shall do will be to make some decent roads.' And of course that set him off thinking about being a King and all the other things he would do and this cheered him up a good deal. He had just settled in his mind what sort of palace he would have and how many cars and all about his private cinema and where the principal railways would run and what laws he would make against beavers and dams and was putting the finishing touches to some schemes for keeping Peter in his place, when the weather changed.

The real antagonist of the story is the White Witch, of course. She is the one seeking to enforce her own vacuum-filling 'solutions' onto the world. The bulk of the story is a chase sequence as she pursues the children across Narnia. This is a classic linear vacuum mechanism: 'What will happen next?' is the ongoing question in a chase or hunt which moves the reader through the tale, event by event.

> 'But that isn't what she'll do first,' said Mrs Beaver, 'not if I know her. The moment that Edmund tells her that we're all here she'll set out to catch us this very night, and if he's been gone about half an hour, she'll be here in about another twenty minutes.'

> 'You're right, Mrs Beaver,' said her husband, 'we must all get away from here. There's not a moment to lose.'

As we have pointed out, linear vacuums are the bare bones of any story, since story-telling began: one event after another, prompted by the question 'What will happen next?' Unfortunately, for many writers linear vacuums are all the vacuums that are employed. Alone, they are not enough. Apart from being driven *through* a story, we need to have our attention *glued to* the story. While we are moving through the chase sequence, our attention is attracted by the character vacuums of poor Edmund, upon whom it gradually dawns that he has chosen the wrong side, and by the mystery vacuum of Aslan the Lion.

When the children meet Aslan, the supreme ally, (in effect the old man with a stick representing as he does the Emperor-Over-Sea) it seems at first that all the vacuums will be imminently filled, equilibrium restored and the tale concluded - and this may very well have been the case in the hands of a lesser story-teller. Lewis has other ideas. He intends to create an even bigger loss, need, desire, through Aslan's sacrifice, thus manufacturing the big character and plot vacuum needed to draw the reader into maximum emotional commitment.

With Aslan gone, we apparently lose everything just when we thought that the battle and the story might be over. This moment is also tangled up with a big moral vacuum: 'What is the right thing to do?' Aslan makes the supreme sacrifice because it is the right thing to do, and the moral vacuum grips us even further.

Susan and Lucy are witnesses to the sacrifice and experience a huge loss:.

> And it was all more lonely and hopeless and horrid than I know how to describe. 'I wonder could we untie him as well?' said Susan presently. But the enemies, out of pure spitefulness, had drawn the cords so tight that the girls could make nothing of the knots. I hope no one who reads this book has been quite as miserable as Susan and Lucy were that night; but if you have been - if you've been up all night and cried till you have no more tears left in you - you will know that there comes in the end a sort of quietness. You feel as if nothing was ever going to happen again. At any rate that was how it felt to these two.

> Hours and hours seemed to go by in this dead calm, and they hardly noticed that they were getting colder and colder.

It takes a giant vacuum to get a giant emotional commitment.

But Lewis isn't writing a Tragedy or an Irony - he wants to produce Joy. Aslan's resurrection fills this core vacuum and removes the final mystery vacuum:

> 'But what does it all mean?' asked Susan when they were somewhat calmer.

> 'It means,' said Aslan, 'that though the Witch knew the Deep Magic, there is a magic deeper still which she did not know: Her knowledge goes back only to the dawn of time. But if she could have looked a little further back, into the stillness and the darkness before Time dawned, she would have read there a different incantation. She would have known that when a willing victim who had committed no treachery was killed in a traitor's stead, the Table would crack and Death itself would start working backwards. And now -'

> 'Oh yes. Now?' said Lucy, jumping up and clapping her hands.

> 'Oh, children,' said the Lion, 'I feel my strength coming back to me. Oh, children, catch me if you can!'

Once the reader is emotionally committed on this scale, the battle that takes place afterwards has meaning; without the commitment, it's just words on a page, a hollow scenario, like a scene from a video game.

It's all the more powerful when the children take up the empty thrones in Cair Paravel because their character vacuums are also filled: Edmund matures into a rounded human being and all the children grow into adult kings and queens:

> These two Kings and two Queens governed Narnia well, and long and happy was their reign. At first much of their time was spent in seeking out the remnants of the White Witch's army and destroying them, and indeed for a long time there would be news of evil things lurking in the wilder parts of the forest - a haunting here and a killing there, a glimpse of a werewolf one month and a rumour of a hag the next. But in the end all that foul brood was stamped out. And they made good laws and kept the peace and saved good trees from being unnecessarily cut down, and liberated young dwarfs and young satyrs from being sent to school, and generally stopped busybodies and interferers and encouraged ordinary people who wanted to live and let live.

As you can see, in an ideal work of fiction, character vacuums (missing parents, wounds, scars and so on) attract readers, but should then unite with simple linear vacuums ('What will happen next?') to produce momentum. Mystery vacuums ('What's really going on?') glue our attention, along with moral vacuums ('What's the right thing to do?') Core vacuums (tapping into basic vacuums and carrying the reader through to the finale) then produce what the reader wants: fulfilment.

The more vacuums, the better, is the usual rule. In Comedies and Epics, we expect vacuums to be filled; in Tragedies and Ironies, vacuums tend to remain unfilled and others are only partially filled or filled in unexpected ways.

Get the reader more worried, more anxious, increase the need. 'Is it unethical to worry a reader by apparently increasing his or her needs?' you ask. The purpose is to achieve emotional commitment - without emotional commitment, the tale is hollow.

Your job as a fiction writer is to create and then fill vacuums (or leave them empty, if you want to produce a tragic or ironic mood).

'If I'm spending all this time encouraging talk about the vacuums of the reader, don't I ever get to speak about what I want to write about?' is another common question at this point. If fiction doesn't generate vacuums that resonate with the needs of readers, it is never going to succeed. It will always fight an uphill battle to get published. Strangely, the truth is that, if this is done right, imaginative ideas will flow more easily and be filled with new meaning. That's because meaning shines out in contrast with all the gaps, emptinesses, needs, desires and losses that are created.

The meaningfulness of fiction deepens as more vacuums are added.

Readers aren't attracted to meaning in any context. They are only attracted to meaning by the vacuums around it. Attempts to convey meaning without vacuums will cause reader attention to drift. This gives us one of the chief axioms of vacuum power:

Loss of interest in readers always always always indicates a weakening of vacuums in the work being read.

The job of a vacuum-generating writer is to boost the vacuums until the reader emotionally commits, not rave on about ideas or something else while the reader slows to a standstill or slides backwards.

Those things that appear to us to be 'dramatic' or 'action-packed' or full of energy in stories are precisely those things that contain vacuums. And vacuums are *contagious*.

In successful fiction, universal vacuums lead to common vacuums which in turn lead to basic vacuums. When a reader arrives at a piece of fiction, they experience, through the mechanism of character vacuums, a universally recognisable loss or need; then those losses or needs grow into emptinesses, desires, mysteries and unknowns through linear vacuums, mystery vacuums, character vacuums, moral vacuums and eventually core vacuums.

If this sequence is followed, readers emotionally commit with almost no effort whatsoever.

Keep talking about ideas, 'character background', exposition, description, or any other attempt to show off 'style', and so on, and a work of fiction risks losing readers.

Epics, then, conclude with social and individual vacuums being filled satisfactorily. Often, though, as we have pointed out, the protagonist's vacuums grow so large within the tale that they are difficult to fill within the constructed stagework of the story and so the protagonist must move to some kind of higher plane: Frodo goes to Valinor; Harry becomes an adult wizard; Luke Skywalker becomes a Jedi; Arthur goes to Avalon to become the 'Once and Future King', and so on.

Chapter Eight:
'Macbeth' - A Case Study

Macbeth is a perfect example of how a Tragedy applies vacuum power.

Traditionally, tragic heroes are said to be motivated by *hamartia*, the in-built 'flaw' which leads an otherwise noble protagonist figure to destruction. This is another way of saying 'character vacuum'. And we find that character vacuums are indeed the main engine which drives Tragedies, *Macbeth* being no exception. Macbeth as a protagonist is normally said to 'suffer' from over-ambition, but in vacuum terms over-ambition would be better stated as a lack of acknowledgement from the society around him.

Shakespeare's understanding of vacuum power gives us a master-class in how to use it to construct a Tragedy in this play.

We begin with the three witches who immediately suggest implicitly and explicitly that the natural order is going to be subverted and our expectations along with it:

Act One

Scene 1

A desert place

(Thunder and lightning. Enter three witches.)

First Witch: When shall we three meet again

In thunder, lightning, or in rain?

Second Witch: When the hurly-burly's done,

When the battles lost and won.

Third Witch: That will be ere set of sun.

First Witch: Where the place?

Second Witch: Upon the heath.

Third Witch: There to meet with Macbeth.

First Witch: I come, Graymalkin.

All: Paddock calls: -anon!

Fair is foul, and foul is fair.

Hover through the fog and filthy air.

(Exeunt)

This first scene creates a powerful mystery vacuum. But our introduction to the eponymous hero himself is far from what our vacuum theory might suggest at first glance. Instead of being a figure who is missing something, he seems to have everything - courage, command of himself and almost superhuman powers are listed among his qualities:

For brave Macbeth - well he deserves that name-

Disdaining fortune, with his brandish'd steel

Which smoked with bloody execution,

Like valour's minion carved out his passage

Till he faced the slave;

Which ne'er shook hands, nor bade farewell to him,

Till he unseam'd him from the nave to the chaps,

And fix'd his head upon our battlements.

Duncan: O valiant cousin! Worthy gentleman!

He appears to be the master of all he surveys - but the point is precisely that he isn't. Someone else is king. Macbeth has a character vacuum which reveals itself after he and his companion meet the witches, who, in terms of vacuum theory, do not so much prophesy that he will become king as delineate Macbeth's inner vacuum for the audience. We glimpse this character vacuum through his first soliloquy:

Macbeth (aside):   Two truths are told,

As happy prologues to the swelling act

Of the imperial theme. - I thank you, gentlemen -

(Aside) This supernatural soliciting

Cannot be ill; cannot be good: if ill,

Why hath it given me earnest of success,

Commencing in a truth? I am thane of Cawdor:

If good, why do I yield to that suggestion

Whose horrid image doth unfix my hair

And make my seated heart knock at my ribs,

Against the use of nature? Present fears

Are less than horrible imaginings:

My thought, whose murder yet is but fantastical,

Shakes so my single state of man that function

Is smother'd in surmise, and nothing is

But what is not.

This inner vacuum gnaws at him within, opening up a gap in his constructed personality - or rather, revealing that his constructed personality *is* an inner vacuum. Like all protagonists, Macbeth is the construct with the most vacuums in the story.

Shakespeare doesn't let up on the development of this character vacuum: the next scene shows us the king, Duncan (the misguided old man with a stick in this Tragedy) granting power and titles to his son, Malcolm. Critical arguments abound over whether this reveals Duncan's lack of judgement as king in overlooking Macbeth as the military leader who has just saved his kingdom, but this is beside the point: dramatically and in terms of vacuum power, what it really does is again highlight Macbeth's inner character vacuum:

Macbeth: (aside) The Prince of Cumberland! that is a step

On which I must fall down, or else o'erleap,

For in my way it lies. Stars, hide your fires;

Let not light see my black and deep desires:

The eye wink at the hand; yet let that be

Which the eye fears, when it is done, to see.

On its own, though, this vacuum is still not strong enough to produce a powerful emotional commitment in the audience. So Shakespeare introduces us to the female companion, the vacuum-laden Lady Macbeth, who is shown literally emptying her soul on stage:

Come, you spirits

That tend on mortal thoughts, unsex me here,

And fill me, from the crown to the toe, top-full

Of direst cruelty! make thick my blood,

Stop up the access and passage to remorse,

That no compunctious visitings of nature

Shake my fell purpose, nor keep peace between

The effect and it! Come to my woman's breasts,

And take my milk for gall, you murdering ministers,

Wherever in your sightless substances

You wait on nature's mischief! Come, thick night,

And pall thee in the dunnest smoke of hell,

That my keen knife see not the wound it makes,

Nor heaven peep through the blanket of the dark,

To cry 'Hold, hold!'

It is her vacuum power, added to Macbeth's own, which tips things over into action, prompting Macbeth to kill the king. Her savage argument with him, during which she paints him as a walking vacuum, not a man at all, ends with Macbeth ending his procrastination:

Lady Macbeth: What beast was't then

That made you break this enterprise to me?

When you durst do it, then you were a man;

And, to be more than what you were, you would

Be so much more the man. Nor time nor place

Did then adhere, and yet you would make both:

They have made themselves, and that their fitness now

Does unmake you. I have given suck and know

How tender 'tis to love the babe that milks me:

I would, while it was smiling in my face,

Have pluck'd my nipple from his boneless gums,

And dash'd the brains out, had I sworn as you

Have done to this.

Macbeth: If we should fail?

Fed emptiness by his wife, Macbeth now has tremendous vacuum power as a character, but to continue to hold the audience's attention and to get the full commitment needed, even this must grow. Macbeth determines to empty himself of humanity even further and visits the witches again. Growing more and more hollow, Macbeth slaughters Macduff's innocent family.

Lady Macbeth becomes such a strong example of walking emptiness - a case of the female companion becoming a personified vacuum if ever there was one - that she sleepwalks in her insanity; after her suicide, Macbeth points out in a soliloquy that he has lost everything and has entered the autumn of his life:

I have lived long enough: my way of life

Is fall'n into the sear, the yellow leaf,

And that which should accompany old age,

As honour, love, obedience, troops of friends,

I must not look to have; but, in their stead,

Curses, not loud but deep, mouth-honour, breath,

Which the poor heart would fain deny, and dare not.

Ultimately, reader commitment is made when every one of the witches' prophecies is found to be a false message, progressing step by step through ever-larger vacuums until we know he really has nothing left:

And be these juggling fiends no more believed,

That palter with us in a double sense;

That keep the word of promise to our ear,

And break it to our hope.

We find all our constructed, archetypal figures present in some form, but wearing Tragic clothes: Duncan, the old man with the stick; Lady Macbeth the female vacuum figure (who doesn't even have a name of her own); Banquo the 'comic' companion; Malcolm the warrior king with the suggestion of duplicity; and Macduff, acting as a shadow protagonist. The antagonists are the witches, filling the protagonist with false hope.

In Tragedy, society's vacuums are filled with restored order and usually a new king, but the individual protagonist's vacuums are not: that's why it's a Tragedy.

Chapter Nine:
'Great Expectations' - A Case Study

In Charles Dickens' Ironic masterpiece *Great Expectations*, it's not difficult to spot our vacuum-laden protagonist. The opening of the novel labours the point that Pip has lost his parents and is living in desolate circumstances:

> My first most vivid and broad impression of the identity of things seems to me to have been gained on a memorable raw afternoon towards evening. At such a time I found out for certain that this bleak place overgrown with nettles was the churchyard; and that Philip Pirrip, late of this parish, and also Georgiana wife of the above, were dead and buried; and that Alexander, Bartholomew, Abraham, Tobias, and Roger, infant children of the aforesaid, were also dead and buried; and that the dark flat wilderness beyond the churchyard, intersected with dikes and mounds and gates, with scattered cattle feeding on it, was the marshes; and that the low leaden line beyond was the river; and that the distant savage lair from which the wind was rushing was the sea; and that the small bundle of shivers growing afraid of it all and beginning to cry, was Pip.

Dickens amplifies this classic character vacuum to further glue our attention to Pip, who, while visiting the graves of his mother, father and siblings, encounters an escaped convict, Magwitch, in the village churchyard. The convict scares Pip into stealing food (and a file to grind away his shackles) from the home he shares with his abusive older sister and her kind husband Joe Gargery, a blacksmith. In this first section of the novel, Dickens works each paragraph to magnify the loss or threat of loss surrounding Pip using one linear vacuum after another, winding up with Pip in absolute terror of his life:

> Since that time, which is far enough away now, I have often thought that few people know what secrecy there is in the young under terror. No matter how unreasonable the terror, so that it be terror. I was in mortal terror of the young man who wanted my heart and liver; I was in mortal terror of my interlocutor with the iron leg; I was in mortal terror of myself, from whom an awful promise had been extracted; I had no hope of

deliverance through my all-powerful sister, who repulsed me at every turn; I am afraid to think of what I might have done on requirement, in the secrecy of my terror.

The next day, soldiers recapture the convict while he is engaged in a fight with another escaped convict; the two are returned to the prison ships and disappear from the reader's radar for the moment, but not before leaving the lingering impression of a mystery connection between the convicts.

Then Dickens sets to work on further mystery and character vacuums to hold our attention. Miss Havisham, a wealthy spinster who wears an old wedding dress and lives in the time-frozen, dilapidated Satis House, asks Pip's Uncle Pumblechook to find a boy to visit. Pip visits Miss Havisham and her adopted daughter Estella, falling in love with Estella on first sight, though both are quite young. Estella is a standard female companion figure, but, given that this is an Irony, she is even more of a walking vacuum, hollowed out by her mentor and empty of any positive emotion:

> Estella was always about, and always let me in and out, but never told me I might kiss her again. Sometimes, she would coldly tolerate me; sometimes, she would condescend to me; sometimes, she would be quite familiar with me; sometimes, she would tell me energetically that she hated me. Miss Havisham would often ask me in a whisper, or when we were alone, 'Does she grow prettier and prettier, Pip?' And when I said yes (for indeed she did), would seem to enjoy it greedily. Also, when we played at cards Miss Havisham would look on, with a miserly relish of Estella's moods, whatever they were. And sometimes, when her moods were so many and so contradictory of one another that I was puzzled what to say or do, Miss Havisham would embrace her with lavish fondness, murmuring something in her ear that sounded like 'Break their hearts my pride and hope, break their hearts and have no mercy!'

Instead of being a vacuum-filler for Pip, Estella acts to increase his character vacuum and his desire for her motivates his decisions throughout the story. Meanwhile, while both Pip and Joe are away from the house, Mrs. Joe is brutally attacked, by an unknown figure (creating another mystery vacuum) leaving her unable to speak or do her work. Biddy - who we recognise would have been a more suitable partner for Pip - is ironically overlooked when she arrives to care for Mrs. Joe.

Four years into Pip's apprenticeship, Mr. Jaggers, a lawyer, fulfilling the Ironic version of the old man with a stick character, approaches him in the village with the news that he has expectations from an anonymous benefactor, with immediate funds to train him in the gentlemanly arts. He will not know the benefactor's name until that person speaks up. Pip is to leave for London in the proper clothes:

'Now you are to understand, secondly, Mr. Pip, that the name of the person who is your liberal benefactor remains a profound secret, until the person chooses to reveal it. I am empowered to mention that it is the intention of the person to reveal it at first hand by word of mouth to yourself. When or where that intention may be carried out, I cannot say; no one can say. It may be years hence. Now, you are distinctly to understand that you are most positively prohibited from making any inquiry on this head, or any allusion or reference, however distant, to any individual whomsoever as the individual, in all the communications you may have with me. If you have a suspicion in your own breast, keep that suspicion in your own breast.'

Dickens thus creates the central mystery vacuum which will power the rest of the novel. Pip assumes that Miss Havisham is his benefactor, a typical Ironic error.

In London, Pip sets up house with Herbert Pocket, the comic companion for this story.

As the novel proceeds, a week after he turns 23 years old, Pip learns in true Ironic style that his benefactor is not Miss Havisham at all but the convict from so long ago, Abel Magwitch. Pip's entire purpose and motivation turns out to have been driven by a false conception.

As long as he is out of England, Magwitch can live, but, a wretched figure driven by his own vacuums and longing to see again the one person who showed him mercy, he returns to see Pip. Meeting Pip again was his motivation for all his success in New South Wales.

This is the resolution of the central mystery vacuum and the point of emotional commitment for the reader. This is followed by the core vacuum, the working out of the battle between Magwitch and Compeyson.

As *Great Expectations* is an Irony, everything goes wrong. Though Pip and Herbert devise a plan to get Magwitch out of England by boat, Pip tells Miss Havisham that he is as unhappy as she can ever have meant him to be, and Estella tells Pip she will marry Bentley Drummle. In a series of mounting vacuums, the plot works itself out; Joe's former journeyman Orlick (a shadow protagonist) seizes Pip, confessing past crimes as he means to kill him; Herbert Pocket and Startop save Pip and prepare for the escape.

On the river, they are met by a police boat carrying Compeyson for identification of Magwitch. Compeyson was the other convict years earlier, and as well, the confidence trickster who wooed and deserted Miss Havisham. Magwitch seizes Compeyson, and they fight in the river. Magwitch survives to be taken by police, seriously injured and dies soon after, sparing an execution.

The rest of the Irony is a sequence of purposely ill-fitting vacuum-fillers and missed opportunities: after Herbert goes to Cairo, Pip falls ill in his rooms; he is confronted with arrest for debt; he returns to propose to Biddy, to find that she and Joe have just married. Dickens isn't trying to produce Joy, but its opposite.

As Magwitch's fortune in money and land is seized by the court, Pip no longer has income. Eleven years later, after working hard in the world, Pip visits the ruins of Satis House and meets Estella, widow to the abusive Bentley Drummle. The scene is set for the resolution of the major character vacuum that has motivated Pip throughout the story. In a variation on Dickens' original bleaker ending, Estella asks Pip to forgive her, assuring him that misfortune has opened her heart and that she now empathises with Pip:

> 'We are friends,' said I, rising and bending over her, as she rose from the bench.

> 'And will continue friends apart,' said Estella.

> I took her hand in mine, and we went out of the ruined place; and, as the morning mists had risen long ago when I first left the forge, so the evening mists were rising now, and in all the

broad expanse of tranquil light they showed to me, I saw no shadow of another parting from her.

Finally, there is some promise of vacuums being filled, though the sentence is still Pip's subjective hope rather than fictive truth: we don't know what happens next, and, in typically Ironic fashion, we are left hanging in an incomplete linear vacuum.

In constructing an Irony, perhaps even moreso than when creating an Epic, then, the emphasis is on vacuums: emptinesses, losses, gaps, mysteries, unknowns. But whereas Epics resolve when most or all of these created vacuums are filled, in Ironies they are left for the most part yawningly open and empty.

That's a recent modern film Epic, a Shakespearian Tragedy, and a Dickensian Irony, all following the same patterns and using character vacuums, linear vacuums, mystery vacuums and core vacuums with varying effects. To prove the point that vacuums are at work in all fiction and in all media, let's take a look at something a bit different for Comedy.

Chapter Ten:
'Friends' - A Case Study

The last remaining quarter of the Wheel of Fiction, Comedy, is an opportunity to investigate an entirely different form of text to show that the principles of vacuum power are quite universal.

Does an American television sit-com also operate on vacuum power?

Friends was an American television sitcom, created by David Crane and Marta Kauffman, which originally aired on NBC from September 22, 1994, to May 6, 2004. It revolved around a circle of friends living in Manhattan. All ten seasons of the show ranked within the top ten of the final television season ratings - it reached the top spot with its eighth season. The series finale on May 6, 2004, was watched by around 52.5 million American viewers, making it the fifth most watched series finale in television history, and the most watched television episode of the 2000s decade.

Friends received positive reviews throughout its run, becoming one of the most popular sit-coms of all time. It was nominated for 62 Primetime Emmy Awards, winning the Outstanding Comedy Series award in 2002 for its eighth season and many other awards, including, in 2014, the Best TV Series of All Time.

If we are correct about the things we have been examining - character, linear, mystery, moral and core vacuums and so forth - we should find plenty of evidence of them in such a successful form of fiction. Let's look at a summary of the series' premise and see if we can tell what to expect.

The overall story of the sit-com is that the main couple, Ross and Rachel, finally get together after ten years of comic mis-matching and laughter-laden misunderstandings.

In the opening episode, character Rachel Green abandons her proposed husband on her wedding day and seeks out childhood friend Monica Geller, a New York City chef. They become roommates. Rachel joins Monica's social circle of single people in their mid-20s:

struggling actor Joey Tribbiani, business professional Chandler Bing, musician and masseuse Phoebe Buffay, and newly-divorced paleontologist Ross Geller, Monica's older brother. Rachel becomes a waitress at Central Perk, a Manhattan coffeehouse where the group frequently gathers. The six also often get together at Monica and Rachel's nearby West Village apartment, or at Joey and Chandler's place across the hall.

Episodes typically depict a range of romantic adventures and career issues with a comedic twist, including Joey auditioning for roles as an actor or Rachel seeking jobs in the fashion industry. The six characters each have many dates and serious relationships, but it is Ross and Rachel's intermittent relationship which is the most often-recurring storyline. During the ten seasons of the show Ross and Rachel repeatedly date and break up; Ross briefly marries someone else; he and Rachel have a child; Chandler and Monica eventually marry each other, and Phoebe marries outside the central group. Frequently recurring characters include Ross and Monica's parents in Long Island, Ross's ex-wife and their son, Central Perk barista Gunther, Chandler's ex-girlfriend Janice, and Phoebe's twin sister Ursula.

According to vacuum theory, each of these six main characters, to work successfully as characters, should be constructed of vacuums - needs, desires, missing items, vulnerabilities, losses or inadequacies. These 'gaps' act to draw in viewer attention and sympathy.

In the case of *Friends*, these things abound.

Character Vacuums in *Friends*

Jennifer Aniston portrays Rachel Green, a fashion enthusiast. Rachel first moves in with Monica in season one after nearly marrying Barry Farber, whom she realises she does not love. So the opening episode plants one big vacuum in its first main character: Rachel's loss of her future, her proposed husband and stability generally (she has no job). Though Rachel dates other men during the series, such as an Italian neighbour, Paolo, her client Joshua Bergin, her assistant Tag or even Joey Tribbiani, it is made clear to the audience that she is unstable in the romantic department - i.e. her inner character vacuum isn't adequately resolved.

Rachel and Ross even have a daughter together named Emma in the episode entitled 'The One Where Rachel Has a Baby, Part Two', but even this apparent vacuum filler is not enough to settle her down. In the final episode of the entire series Ross and Rachel finally confess their love for each other: Rachel gives up a job in Paris (also a potential but inadequate vacuum filler for her) and the show closes with its central character vacuum - the 'missing' love between Ross and Rachel - resolved and fulfilled.

Courteney Cox portrays Monica Geller, a chef, known for her perfectionist, bossy and control-obsessed attitude, and competitive nature. These traits are established as her character vacuums - her inability to relax and later her anxieties about her childhood - Monica is often jokingly teased by the others for having been overweight as a child, especially by her brother Ross. Monica and Chandler Bing later start a relationship after spending a night with each other in London, leading to their marriage in season seven and adoption of twins at the end of the series. In this way - finding a stable partner and being able to become a mother - Monica's initial character vacuum is addressed, to be immediately replaced by anxieties about her inability to have children of her own. The adoption - after a series of comic mishaps - means that, by the end of the series, she achieves fulfilment.

Phoebe Buffay, portrayed by Lisa Kudrow, is an eccentric masseuse and self-taught musician who lived in uptown New York with her mother until her mother committed suicide. This is a vacuum of magnitude which is played for comic effect by having Phoebe be scatter-brained but street-smart. She writes and sings her own quirky songs, accompanying herself on the guitar and is childlike and innocent in disposition, using her past misfortunes such as her mother's suicide as sympathy ploys. Her fulfilling marriage in the show's final season comes after several other failed relationships which come close to, but fail to resolve, her character needs.

Matthew Perry portrays Chandler Bing, an executive in statistical analysis and data reconfiguration for a large multinational corporation who later quits his job (creating a vacuum of instability temporarily) and becomes a junior copywriter at an advertising agency. On the surface, Chandler's life surrounded by friends and with enough money and a good lifestyle, suggests less vacuums in his character but as the series goes on it becomes apparent that he has a peculiar family history: he is the son of an erotic novelist mother and a gay, cross-dressing Las Vegas star father. This challenging background has led to his central character vacuum, his uncertainty about himself, which he demonstrates through his sarcastic sense of humour and bad luck in relationships. Chandler's marriage to Monica in season seven, and their adoption of twins by the end of the series, acts to fulfil his needs.

David Schwimmer portrays Ross Geller, Monica Geller's older brother, a paleontologist working at New York's Museum of Natural History, and later at New York University. Ross is outwardly a sweet-natured man of good humour, but has an ongoing character vacuum: he is often clumsy and socially awkward. This social inadequacy leads to three failed or abortive marriages during the series: to Rachel, Emily, and Carol, a lesbian who is also the mother of his son, Ben. His failed love life is contributed to by the underlying vacuum of paranoia and jealousy in relationships which certain episodes reveal in a comedic stagework, and his divorces become a point of humour within the series.

Struggling actor and food lover Joey Tribbiani, played by Matt LeBlanc, becomes famous as the series unfolds for his role on soap opera *Days of Our Lives* as Dr. Drake Ramoray, but Joey as a character is a simple-minded womanizer with many short-term girlfriends. His innocence, coupled with a caring, and well-intentioned attitude, reveals less of a character vacuum than any of the others and he experiences less character change or fulfilment than any of the others by the end of the series. (Interestingly, after *Friends* concluded, his character is then given his own comedy show, *Joey*, indicating that there is something about him as a character that is unresolved.)

Audience Viewpoint

Comedy characters, then, have character vacuums just as characters do in Epics, Tragedies or Ironies, though these are viewed in a more light-hearted way because they are comically exaggerated. Shifted slightly, each of the *Friends* characters' vacuums look grimmer: all have relationship issues and all suffer from psychological problems of one kind or another; all have potentially traumatic backgrounds to some degree, with Phoebe's family tragedy probably being the worst. How then does Comedy deal with character vacuums which in another genre would be the substance of grief, mental disturbance or much drama?

Partly by having an ensemble approach. Comedies often deflect the intense vacuum power associated with protagonists in Epics, Tragedies and in particular Ironies by having more than one protagonist. Though it is clear that the central thread tying together the series as a whole is the relationship between Ross and Rachel - making them the closest things to the show's protagonists as we get - the truth is that every episode of *Friends* features a balance of focus between the six major characters which acts to alleviate the seriousness or gravity of each of their personal vacuums.

In Comedies, character and plot vacuums are also changed somewhat by the placement of the audience. It is not by accident that television situation comedies are often 'filmed before a live audience' or use 'canned laughter' to prompt audience reaction at home. This mechanism acts to extrovert the audience from the action - we are constantly aware of the presence of others like us, 'watching' the events before us. That means we don't take them too seriously.

A simple experiment can highlight this: take any episode of *Friends* and remove the 'live audience' or 'canned laughter' element. The events immediately take a more serious turn in our eyes. For example, Ross's outrage at his work colleague's accidental consumption of Ross's favourite sandwich in one episode is intended to be perceived as funny and our laughter is prompted by the live audience soundtrack. However, take that prompt away and, while the scene is still amusing, we grow more concerned for Ross's mental state.

Conversely, as part of the experiment, take any dark horror film from the Ironic quarter of our division of genres and play a canned laughter soundtrack alongside the scenes of impending death or terror on screen - and we instantly cannot take the events we are watching seriously at all, or the scene becomes bizarre and unsettling in a very different way. Stanley Kubrick made use of this discordance in films such as *A Clockwork Orange* or *Doctor Strangelove*: at moments of the most severe psychological impact, such as a rape scene or the beginning of a nuclear war, inappropriately comic or light-hearted music is played. The effect is eerie - our immersion into the seriousness of what is happening on screen is interrupted and made strangely disturbing.

Comic Archetypes

Do any of these comic characters fit our character archetypes? Is there a 'protagonist' and an 'antagonist'? Is anyone fulfilling the role of the 'old man with a stick'?

If Comedies are often based on an ensemble and don't really have as defined a 'protagonist', then what happens to the fixed roles we have found in other genres?

Let's assume Ross is as much of a protagonist as we are going to find in *Friends* - then Rachel is his 'female companion' and Joey and Phoebe fall into place to some degree as comic companions, in a world where every major character is constructed to be comic to some degree.

Monica, who bosses her brother around and asserts manic control regularly could be allocated the 'warrior king' role. That leaves Chandler as the 'old man with a stick', which hardly fits unless we accept that it is his sarcasm and tendency to view situations from the outside which comes closest to the activities we would associate with that particular figure. It's all very tentative and shifting because of the ensemble nature of the series, but the archetypes are present to some extent.

What about an antagonist? In *Friends*, as an ensemble, most of the constructed characters have their own antagonists throughout the show's many episodes and triumph over them in various ways. That usually forms the basis of each episode's plot, in effect.

In Comedies generally, as in other genres, the 'antagonist' is someone who is forwarding their own agenda, blindly and mechanically seeking dominance of one kind or another. Thus Egeus in *A Midsummer Night's Dream* wants to use Athens' law to control his daughter's future; Lady Catherine de Burgh in *Pride and Prejudice* asserts social conventions in order to try to have her way; Potter, the 'scurvy old spider' banker in *It's a Wonderful Life* calls the sheriff to arrest George Bailey so that he can dominate the town of Bedford Falls.

Antagonists in Comedy, then, are much the same as antagonists anywhere.

Plot Vacuums in Comedy

Linear vacuums underlie the whole principle of the 'joke' in which a story is told with an unexpected and comic 'punchline' or outcome. A joke needs a specific and well-defined narrative structure to have the effect of making people laugh. Jokes normally take the form of stories, usually with dialogue. The punchline reveals to the listener that there has all along been a second, conflicting meaning - or, in vacuum terms, the punchline suddenly reveals a vacuum which the listener has not been aware of until that moment, and fills it in an unexpected way.

These can be very succinct and are often one-liners - for example, the now-famous comic statement 'Velcro - what a rip off'. In this simple example, the contextual meaning of the words 'rip off', usually indicating that a customer has been defrauded of value, conflict with the other, simpler meaning of the words, indicating what velcro actually does physically. The listener did not expect there to be a convergence of these two meanings, and thus responds with laughter, the normal human response when a vacuum that was not suspected is filled in an unpredictable way.

Of course, any joke dismantled in this way isn't funny. The essence of humour is the *surprise* one gets from the unexpected exposure of, and filling of, a vacuum.

Take the other one-liner 'I'd give my right hand to be ambidextrous': the idiomatic 'I'd give my right hand', normally taken as a cliché expressing a serious commitment, is suddenly shown to have a second, equally applicable and more obvious meaning in the joke's second half. The listener reacts with a smile - a subdued form of laughter - recognising the hidden vacuum and how it was filled.

Word meanings play a key role in humour of this kind. Definitions are assumed and then quickly revealed to be unsuspected vacuums - gaps, into which other definitions then flow. Puns of course demonstrate this in action by their nature - playing one definition of a word off against another to create that tiny 'fulfilment moment' of recognition.

Humorous forms which are *not* jokes include involuntary humour, situational humour, practical jokes, stand-up comedy, anecdotes, and slapstick or purely visual humour. All of these depend on vacuums - unknowns, gaps, missing things. The situational comedy used by many stand-ups, for example, rests upon the comic's cleverness in spotting a vacuum in people's lives. A comedian relates what happens in a household where children are growing up as opposed to the same events in a household with no children: those with children recognise the situation, which they formerly considered a private matter, unknown to others (vacuum), suddenly exposed and played out on stage (fulfilment); those with no children, having no data on what life is like with them (vacuum), imagine what it must be like from the comedian's antics (fulfilment).

Of course, stand-up comics, comedians and slapstick work with precise comic timing and rhythm in their performance, relying as much on actions as on the verbal punchline to evoke laughter, but this begs a question: what is comic timing?

Comic timing is the creation of a vacuum - a need, an emptiness, an expectation - and its exact but unexpected fulfilment.

Practical jokes and purely visual humour similarly hide a vacuum in front of us and then play it out with an unexpected outcome.

The big difference between Comedy and Tragedy or Irony is that we as an audience or reader are 'in on the joke'. We can see the vacuums that are normally hidden from the participants and players on the stage. Bottom's conceit in *A Midsummer Night's Dream* isn't apparent to him or to anyone else on stage but it is very clear to us; Mr. Collin's sycophancy in *Pride and Prejudice* is plain to us as readers, but invisible to him even to the end. Jane Austen makes the most of this in her novels to suggest character subtleties - small, partly concealed or innocent vacuums, needs, lacks, gaps, which she permits the reader to glimpse but hides from the constructed person themselves. Only the wisest characters in Austen novels - Darcy, Mr. Bennett, Mr. Knightley, Captain Wentworth - are given the gift of being able to see clearly the foibles of others, and to be tactful and discreet with that knowledge.

Characters in Comedy are only permitted to be aware of their own character vacuums for comic effect. In *Friends*, Ross's social awkwardness frustrates him and spoils many potential relationships for him, but makes us laugh: we get to see it 'from the outside', in effect, not having to suffer it. In Tragedies or Ironies, on the other hand, characters suffer from their failings and we are led to suffer with them, not being permitted the perspective that comes with Comedy. If

A Midsummer Night's Dream was re-written into a Tragedy, Bottom would see how he has destroyed his own life with his own character; if *Pride and Prejudice* became an Irony, Mr. Collins would be trapped in an empty, introverted world of his own making.

So plot vacuums in Comedy are heavily associated with character vacuums that motivate action or inaction. A joke or piece of situational humour or a practical joke has a linear vacuum quality to it - 'What will happen next?' being the primary question prompted by most humorous situations. Comedies don't usually have many mystery vacuums - or if they do, the audience knows the answers and the characters are the ones in mystery. All the farces with their cases of mistaken identity, misunderstood events, or mis-timed arrivals and departures are constructed of mystery vacuums which the audience plainly sees unfolding before them but which are hidden from the players. Watch any Charlie Chaplin silent comedy and you will immediately see set-ups - situations which are laden with vacuums for the characters that we as an audience delight in knowing all about beforehand.

Returning to *Friends*, we can see that Ross's relationship with Rachel is going to crash and burn so many times because we can clearly see her instability and his insecurities; we know that Monica and Chandler are going to argue and disagree about something because we know all about her mania and his self-doubt; we can grasp immediately that Phoebe and Joey are going to have difficulty in certain situations because of their audience-visible comic flaws.

Comedy is Tragedy turned inside out: instead of 'tragic flaws' being suffered internally and exposed to an audience through soliloquys, 'comic flaws' are obvious to everyone but the characters themselves. One attracts our pity; the other, our laughter.

Core Vacuums in Comedy

Core vacuums are what the story is really all about - what is the central plot thread which is at work all the time, leading things to a full resolution? What is the Big Question to which the author's message is the answer?

A core vacuum, hinted at by the 'old man with a stick' construct in Epics, Tragedies and Ironies, takes full effect when linear vacuums and mystery vacuums have done their work in obtaining emotional commitment from the reader. Character, linear and mystery vacuums make us care and engage our attention so that we are actually emotionally concerned enough to find out how things work out. It's the same for Comedies. In *A Midsummer Night's Dream* our sympathies are acquired by character, linear and to some degree mystery vacuums (the fairies' magic being a kind of mystery) so that we want to see how the characters end up and even how the workers' play at the end turns out; in *Pride and Prejudice* we are emotionally committed to Lizzy and Darcy by character, linear, mystery and moral vacuums ('Who is right, Wickham or Darcy?') to want things to resolve in the last chapter. But the Big Question, the core vacuum in most Comedies is simply will the central characters get together in marriage - or some similar socially acceptable union?

If we hadn't had our sympathies aroused and engaged in this way, Ross and Rachel's final coming together would mean little to us; the weddings at the end of *A Midsummer Night's Dream* would be hollow and of little concern; Lizzy's marriage to Darcy would simply be an emotionless event. Because we are emotionally embroiled, these moments of fulfilment for imaginary, constructed characters on the screen, on stage or on the page carry weight and have an effect. They are fulfilling.

And that's what you want to do as a writer: create fulfilment.

Comedy, then, is transparent; its vacuums are visible. We are drawn in mainly by exaggerated character vacuums which we see from the outside, and led forward by plot vacuums which are obvious and even predictable to us. And so we laugh and celebrate, rather than cry or tremble or rage.

Chapter Eleven:
A Summary of Character and Plot Vacuums

In each of our four broad genres, then - Epics like modern blockbuster film *Captain America: The Winter Soldier*, Tragedies like Shakespeare's *Macbeth*, Ironies like Dickens' classic Victorian novel *Great Expectations* and Comedies like American television sit-com *Friends* - vacuums are at work.

Character vacuums use the absence of some key quality in a constructed person to attract our attention, then plot vacuums of various kinds lead us forward to some kind of fulfilment (in Comedies and Epics), or calculated lack of fulfilment (in Tragedies or Ironies).

Most writers are desirous of one key thing: they want to create an effect, usually an emotional effect, upon readers. You now have the basic tools to do this. Using the principles described above, you should be magnifying all the risks, threats, losses and emptinesses in your constructed people and in your existing stories: the need for self knowledge and family, the longing for an easier life, the desire for love or peace the injustice of events, and so on.

Work on the vacuums that will pull the reader closer and closer to an emotional commitment to your work. Keep talking about your ideas, images, thoughts, and so on, and you risk losing readers. They will want to know some of those, but again, only insofar as this relates to *needs*. Talk too much about things other than needs and, in the reader's mind, things slow right down.

You can see this with young children, learning to read or listening to stories. Long passages of description or exposition are 'boring' and are skipped where possible. What younger readers want is action, movement, changes - all the things created by vacuums.

Linear vacuums - based on the question 'What happens next?' - can lure in even the least interested reader if they are constructed with skill. They utilise the simple sequential nature of narrative itself to get things going and get pace raised and momentum strengthened. A chase or a hunt is enough. The popularity of the disaster movie in the 1970s was built on this straightforward linear vacuum structure: would the building collapse? Would the ship sink? Would the people escape?

Character construction doesn't begin by describing everything there is to know about a character in the hope that they will spring to life. Instead of going into great detail, outline the problems they are currently experiencing, the difficulties that they have had with prior events, the threat looming if they don't get something right, and so forth.

Needless to say by now, character and plot vacuums exert a force on the reader and virtually drag them to turn the page.

Drone on about characters, the details of how good they are, and so on, and readers switch off. Most of the 'tricks' that writers come up with to try to make their fiction more engaging are in fact attempted solutions based on an ignorance or only partial awareness of the principles you are learning about here. The huge investment of time that takes place in compiling works large and small, all around the globe, is futile in the absence of these missing basics.

The ideal thing is to find or create a vacuum which is strong enough to overcome any obstacles, pulling the reader and the moment of fulfilment together.

If you don't have enough readers, work on vacuums.

If you don't have enough emotional commitment, work on vacuums.

If you don't have enough of anything, work on vacuums.

'So where can I actually mention my message?' you ask.

Messages - moments of fulfilment (or, in Tragedies and Ironies, carefully crafted moments when fulfilment does not occur) - should only be hinted at when the reader is emotionally committed enough.

This is a clear point. The reader will not necessarily accept the message of a text on an emotional or spiritual level until needs and wants have sufficiently glued him or her to the page.

Lewis doesn't have Mr. Beaver mention Aslan until we are sufficiently glued to the characters of *The Lion, the Witch and the Wardrobe* for such a mention to have any kind of resonance with us.

George Lucas doesn't have Obi Wan talk about the Force or the battle between the Empire and the Rebellion until we are attracted enough by the character vacuums of Luke Skywalker in *Star Wars: A New Hope* for what Obi Wan is saying to have any impact.

Tolkien doesn't have Gandalf hint at higher powers at work in the universe of *The Lord of the Rings* until we have been adequately drawn in by character and mystery vacuums to care.

The Marvel screenwriters don't have Nick Fury mention 'The Avengers Initiative' until right at the end of the credits for the first *Iron Man* movie, by which time we actually like Tony Stark and have seen the character vacuums which motivate him.

And, as we have pointed out earlier, it's normally the 'old man with a stick' figure who hints at fulfilment: Mr. Beaver, Obi Wan Kenobi, Gandalf and Nick Fury all act out that role in each of the pieces of fiction mentioned. Is that a fluke or coincidence? No, there are plenty of other examples.

It's Clark Kent's foster-father who hints at the real meaning of Superman's arrival on Earth in Richard Donner's film *Superman 1* (and it's his real father who outlines the Bigger Picture); it's Atticus who hints at a longer term social justice in *To Kill a Mockingbird*; it's Jaggers who reveals the strange unfolding of fates in *Great Expectations*; it's Professor Godbole who gives us clues as to the meaning of everything in *A Passage to India;* it's the mysterious Inspector who lays out the social themes and consequences of inaction explicitly in J. B. Priestley's *An Inspector Calls*.

One lets the reader or viewer glimpse the message or inner meaning or moment of fulfilment through the figure who represents the 'bigger picture' in some way. But don't linger there - get the reader steered back onto vacuums as soon as possible.

The fiction writer's job is bringing the reader and the message together in an exact match *in such a way that the reader cares what happens* and thus takes the message on board. The result for the reader can be a far-reaching re-orientation.

The key to putting a reader at ease is to find and clarify actual vacuums. The real skill in fiction writing is being able to easily guide the reader's in and out and around character and plot vacuums so that a reader grows more and more connected, giving him or her the feeling of being a part of the story.

The Magnitude of Vacuums

One piece of very good news is this: vacuums are interconnected. Any desire or need for something may indicate a desire or need for a bigger, deeper thing. We covered this to some degree earlier in talking about basic vacuums, common vacuums, universal vacuums and so on. Now you can see that the most effective pieces of fiction make the most of this escalating scale in drawing the reader in.

Think of it in terms of the following diagram.

A character's apparently innocent and small need should connect to a deeper desire which in turn may lead to a more fundamental need. These things ought to occur in a pattern with connections between them. That is what gives a great story its ever-increasing 'pulling power'.

Epic hero Luke Skywalker has an initial character vacuum: an undefined teenage restlessness, a wanting to break away from the constraints of having to work on his uncle's farm. It's a universal vacuum - most readers will recognise it, teenager or not. This then quickly links in to an urgent need to recover R2-D2, the droid who has escaped and made off into the desert of the planet Tatooine. Once Luke meets Obi Wan Kenobi, the 'old man with a stick' (light sabre) who outlines the core vacuum of the story, and then sees his foster family slain, Luke taps into a larger underlying need: the need to fight against the Empire and become a Jedi, like his father before him. This distills into the core vacuum of the tale.

Macbeth is the Tragic version. He begins with a world-weary restlessness, mental images which 'doth unfix' his hair. This is stirred into action by the witches and his wife who tap into his deeper desire to become king. Once crowned, he realises that he has an even more fundamental craving to be secure in his new-found power, and finally, in the tragic unravelling of the witches' false prophecies, we see his world - and his character vacuums - exposed and unfulfilled.

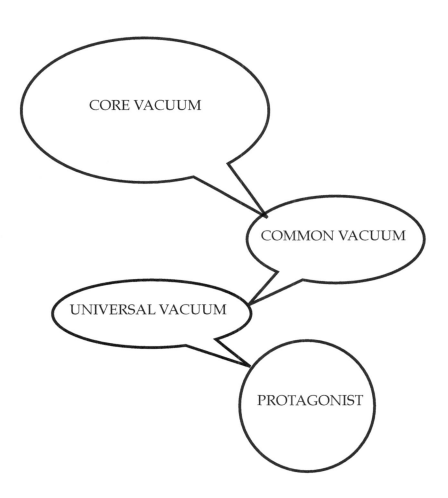

Pip can be an Ironic example of the same escalating progression of vacuums. In *Great Expectations*, at first he is a young boy desiring only to escape his next beating. This quickly becomes a desire for Estella, linked to a desire to be a gentleman. Then he has a greater need to defend and help his benefactor, which culminates in a battle of life and death and love, with an ironically ambiguous ending.

As far as Comedy is concerned, we see *Pride and Prejudice*'s Elizabeth Bennett's mild pining for more contentment in her family rise in magnitude to become her dissatisfaction with Mr. Darcy, which then proceeds exponentially into a quest to save her family's honour.

Stories use this rising scale, this growing void, this swelling of emptinesses to draw the reader into the tale more and more. Core vacuums are inevitably to do with the deepest and widest cravings or needs - they go beyond the individual usually, and become the need for social transformation or moral progress. Readers initially would not perhaps have paid much attention to them, but are compelled to by the power generated by character and plot vacuums.

Your core vacuum is always going to be a basic vacuum, where the stakes are highest.

In *The Lord of the Rings*, the whole world is imperilled by the rise of Sauron, the Dark Lord.

In *Star Wars*, it's the Empire that threatens freedom across the galaxy.

In the *Harry Potter* series, ordinary human life is under threat from the dark wizards.

In *Captain America: The Winter Soldier*, all the citizens of the world are at risk from the fascist organisation, Hydra.

But we only really care about what happens in these larger conflicts because we have been led up through a series of linear, mystery, moral and character vacuums until we are attached to the causes involved.

In Tragedies, the stakes are equally high: Scotland is menaced by the psychotic Macbeth; ancient Britain by the demented Lear.

In Ironies, the stakes can be more internalised but still great, and the novel carries social implications: Pip's life, sanity and happiness collapse in *Great Expectations* but the whole judicial system of Victorian times comes under scrutiny; in *A Passage to India*, the focus is on the individual characters of Aziz and Adela Quested but the nature of the British presence in India is thrown into question.

In Comedies or Romances, the field broadens out once again to include a social implication: in *Pride and Prejudice*, the whole Bennett family's long-term welfare is what is at stake; in *A Midsummer Night's Dream*, it is the seasons themselves that have broken down and need repairing.

These larger, core vacuums are contacted through the lesser vacuums which precede them. Fiction writers who can establish links between lesser, specific vacuums and larger core vacuums engage more readers more powerfully.

A work of fiction which fully utilised vacuum power would be both a dream to read as well as very effective at fulfilment. But as a creative work resists using vacuum power, its attraction goes down. Instead of creating or discovering vacuums which both enable better designed characters as well as smoother and faster plot progression, reading a piece of fiction without vacuum power becomes a struggle.

Revisiting the Antagonist

In fiction, what is a key mechanism is used by authors to increase vacuum power until they tap into the basic level - core vacuums - and get maximum emotional commitment?

The primary vehicle used by successful authors to increase the vacuum power in a story is the antagonist.

We have redefined a 'protagonist' as *that constructed character who acts as the primary focus of vacuums in any successful story*. We have seen that, in a huge range of stories of various kinds, the central figure is a construction made of vacuums, whose losses, needs and gaps grow proportionately throughout the tale, until, towards the end, the character often sacrifices his or her own life, or comes close before being miraculously rescued. In Comedies and Epics, the character 'returns from death' and the vacuum is filled; in Tragedies and Ironies, the vacuum often remains empty and overwhelming.

What, then, of the antagonist?

If our definition of 'protagonist' is reasonably accurate, we should expect the definition of the antagonist to be more or less its opposite. An antagonist should be *that constructed character whose actions produce vacuums on an increasing gradient, magnifying them for the protagonist.*

Furthermore, antagonists seem universally incapable of recognising a vacuum for what it is - a genuine need, basic, common or universal - and this is their downfall.

In *The Lord of the Rings*, we first glimpse Sauron as the Dark Lord whose effect is to create mental conflict in various Ring-bearers from afar. This power then extends into sending the projected vacuums of the Nine Riders - empty, haunted vacuum figures whose souls have long been consumed - against the Fellowship of the Ring. As the forces of good muster against him, Sauron refuses to contemplate that there could be any gap or chink in his armour. He sets about conquering Middle Earth, right up until the Ring is destroyed in the Cracks of Doom and the whole edifice he has constructed collapses. His inability to recognise vacuums leads to his destruction.

In *Star Wars: A New Hope*, the Grand Moff Tarkin and his assistant Darth Vader - who has been drained of life and turned into a cyborg - cannot admit that there might be any kind of weakness in the Death Star, the Dark Side of the Force, or the Imperial Fleet, until the moment when Luke exploits the flaw in the Death Star's plans. In later *Star Wars* films, the Emperor likewise denies any possibility of defeat until Luke persists in seeing the good - or the deep need for repentance - in his father, and Vader throws the Emperor over a rail and into oblivion. None of these antagonists saw the vacuum that was right in front of them.

In the *Harry Potter* series, Voldemort - who at first is no more than a discomfort for Harry but later takes frightening corporeal form using the emptiness in others - and the dark wizards are simply incapable of seeing the strand of virtue which has taken shape right under their noses through the workings of Dumbledore, Snape and Harry, leading to their defeat.

In *Captain America: The Winter Soldier*, Hydra leader Pierce - and his ally the Winter Soldier whose mind has been turned into a vacuum - fails to allow for the structural weakness in the heli-carriers which make it possible for a small team to infiltrate the vessels and undermine Hydra's whole strategy.

This pattern continues in any of the genres.

In Tragedies, Macbeth, who progressively becomes his own antagonist, fails to see his own blindness until the last scene; Lear doesn't glimpse the truth about what has been happening until his last appearance on stage.

In an Irony like *Great Expectations*, Miss Havisham tries to create a walking vacuum in Estella, and use it to break men's hearts. She doesn't see what she is doing until it is too late. Dickens shows her no mercy - her failure to recognise vacuums results in her fiery death.

In Comedies or Romances, antagonists comically remain blind to their personal vacuums (though, as we have seen, the audience is privy to them). Note too that antagonists usually have no sense of humour - that's because humour rests on the use of vacuums, minor and major, as we have seen.

Trying to ignore or suppress vacuums as antagonists do has the opposite effect eventually: the vacuums grow so great and urgent that they become desperate, core vacuums which power the final part of any tale. Whether it is the One Ring (in *The Lord of the Rings*), the Death Star (in *Star Wars: A New Hope*), the Deathly Hallows (in the *Harry Potter* series), the Zola algorithm (in *Captain America: The Winter Soldier*), the witches' prophecies (in *Macbeth*), Estella (in *Great Expectations*) or the power of the law in Athens (in *A Midsummer Night's Dream*), all the devices of an antagonist eventually collapse because they have failed to spot the flaw which was always going to undermine them, and which the protagonist was always going to exploit.

As we know from the world of dentistry, a slight twinge of discomfort in a tooth, if suppressed, can grow worse until eventually serious pain-killers are needed and then massive dental work. Trying to suppress a real and underlying need only worsens things. In fiction terms, this means that those characters who deny or can't see the power of vacuums - we might call them the 'vacuum suppressors' - are giving a clue to their greatest weakness: they deny vacuums and thus expose themselves to defeat as soon as the tiniest one is located.

Vacuums grow in power the more they are denied.

Any denial of need or attempt to conceal it with substitutes, any rejection of vacuums through manically building a world around them, will eventually crumble and collapse. All it will take will be the slightest crack, the smallest sign of real emptiness, and the whole edifice will crash to ruin.

The denied vacuum is usually right at the heart of an antagonist's 'empire', and will manifest itself as the thing that they use to try to overpower the people around them. The One Ring, the Death Star, the Deathly Hallows, the Zola algorithm, the witches' prophecies, the Athenian law - all could be defined as denied vacuums. They all have some weakness in their heart that is critically flawed. But their creators, the antagonists, or those who believe in these things, can't see it or refuse to acknowledge it.

The protagonist represents, from the antagonist's point of view, a growing need which is eventually going to expose and destroy the artifice which the antagonist has created. Thus Luke's progression from teenage restlessness to embryonic Jedi destroys the Death Star; Frodo's development from homesick hobbit to saviour of Middle Earth undermines Sauron's dark empire; Captain America's growth from displaced war veteran to new American symbol is what unravels Hydra, and so on.

Vacuum power - the skilled use of needs, desires, emptinesses, losses in characters and plots - is what drives successful fiction.

Chapter Twelve:
The Secrets of Attention

Here is another useful analogy to help you harness the latent vacuum power in your fiction.

If you have grasped the basics of vacuums - the gaps, losses, needs, desires, emptinesses and things that are missing, which motivate characters and plots, and in doing so pull readers into committing to texts - a sensible next question would be 'What exactly is it that is being sucked into the vacuum?'

And the answer is 'Attention'.

Imagine that the thing we call 'attention' was a plasma, surrounding a person and more or less under that person's control. Picture a person walking around surrounded by a vague cloud of 'attention plasma'.

Right now, in this analogy, your own 'attention plasma' forms a cloud around you, with some of it flowing towards the page as you're reading this sentence.

What's making it flow?

The vacuum between you and the page - your desire to learn what is written here.

Think of attention as a hypothetical substance which people generate and to some degree control, but which is also susceptible to vacuums that they create or which are present in the environment. It's only an analogy, but as you will see, it's a powerful and useful one.

This 'attention plasma' is susceptible to all kinds of vacuums that we already know about: external, internal, positive, negative.

Attention can be described as plasma-like when vague. It floats around, aimless and without focus, subject to the lightest whims.

Like plasma, though, when the temperature drops or other forces are brought to bear, it becomes more like liquid: it begins to coalesce, to become slightly more definite, and it starts to flow.

As we know, flowing liquid can be directed and channeled. It pools, it gathers, it swirls around things.

When attention fixates, it becomes solid.

These states match the sequence of a successful piece of fiction.

Initially, protagonists have little or no idea of their real needs. Their attention is a thin, swirling plasma, not focused on anything in particular. This mirrors the attention of the reader at the beginning of any tale.

As character vacuums become apparent and plot vacuums manifest themselves, attention 'liquifies', becoming slightly more defined but still loose and ethereal.

As vacuums magnify and needs become desperate, attention cascades towards the object of desire, ready to be frozen to it or around it in the moment of fulfilment.

Using this analogy, all any piece of fiction has to do is convert plasma-like attention to liquid and then solidify it around its message, its moment of fulfilment, to be successful.

Readers who are managed in this way embrace messages wholeheartedly; they 'solidify' around them; they experience the magic of fulfilment and the fiction produces the effect it was designed to produce.

Dispersed attention is plasma-like in nature, superficial and wandering. Becoming aware of something missing, a need or vacuum, it chills to liquid and then freezes.

Right now, each person on the planet has some attention on vacuums that have been generated by his or her environment. This is almost what it is to be human. And that's partly why it is intensely useful to you as a fiction writer. If everyone is affected by this attention phenomenon, then it must respond to universal laws and can be acted upon in certain ways. Attention can be left to float around, or it can be directed and channelled.

How can attention be directed and channelled exactly?

With the things we call 'characters'.

Characters draw in attention from readers in various ways, and along various model lines, as we have seen: you can have central vacuum constructs or protagonists, and you can have companion vacuum constructs - a female companion, warrior companion, comic companion and so forth. Then you can have a constructed figure who bridges the reader over into the plot vacuums: the 'old man with a stick'.

Plot vacuums then draw the reader's attention along lines ('What will happen next?'), into mysteries ('What is going on?'), and into moral questions ('What's right?') all the time aiming to increase the reader's commitment so that by the time the core vacuum is approached, sufficient momentum has been built up and the reader will then complete the story and gain fulfilment.

All stories employ these tools in one way or another; successful stories do so more successfully.

Good fiction is a series of steps which takes the potential reader's vague, wandering, unfixed attention and cools it into a more liquid form which is then channelled and directed towards an even more defined need until it eventually coalesces around a message of fulfilment, in an Epic or a Comedy, or, if it's a Tragedy or an Irony, the message of unfulfilment.

Attention, just like water, in a liquid form can be directed more easily. A well-constructed piece of fiction is engineered to have channels in place to make sure that this liquid attention is captured and directed properly. That's largely what this book is about - developing and implementing those channels.

A reader progresses from having vague awareness of need to a more defined and focused need, to an eventual satisfaction of that need.

Fiction takes gas, if you like, and transforms it into stone.

The iceberg that sank the Titanic was once a cloud.

The most successful works of fiction in the world are machines for converting the plasma-like attention of potential readers into solid fulfilment.

Vacuum Patterns

When enough character, linear, moral and mystery vacuums have served their purpose and you have grasped the reader's attention with them, it's time to switch over to the core vacuum, the Bigger Picture.

However, the core vacuum is usually outlined, as we have seen, early in the story. The figure of the old man with the stick has the role of sketching it out and thus giving us the basic shape of the work. Gandalf talks about the background to the One Ring in the second chapter of *The Lord of the Rings*; Obi Wan Kenobi lays out the backstory of the *Star Wars* saga in *A New Hope*; and so on.

At first, this is just a glimpse. It doesn't become the primary vacuum in most stories until later, when more character and plot vacuums have made sure that the reader is emotionally committed. Then the switch to 'core vacuum power' can be made.

In *The Lord of the Rings* this happens when Frodo makes the decision to journey alone into Mordor; in *Star Wars: A New Hope* it's when Luke decides to switch off his targeting computer in the final run at the Death Star; in *Captain America: The Winter Soldier* this is when Captain America broadcasts to the SHIELD crew that he is fighting for freedom. It's a 'goosebump' moment - and the goosebumps indicate the solidification beginning to occur around an approaching moment of fulfilment.

Pip could have decided to give up on Magwitch and reject his situation entirely. Instead, he sticks with him, leading to the dramatic climax of the story.

Macbeth leaves it right until the final scene before he decides to persist - 'Lay on, Macduff, and damned be him that first cries 'Hold, enough!' - despite knowing that he will fail. The core vacuum can be short, but drives the reader straight towards fulfilment once it arrives.

At the same time, the original need or emptiness within the protagonist, his or her character vacuum, is reasserted or validated. In a well-worked out Epic or Comedy, the filling of the core vacuum will also fill or partially fill the character vacuum of the protagonist. In a Tragedy or Irony, the core vacuum is revealed as dooming the protagonist's character to forever be incomplete and unfulfilled.

Epics tend to have expected vacuums based on the traditional character constructs described above and plot structures of stories that we have seen examples of. These vacuums are then filled in various ways: the protagonist 'finds himself'; the female companion 'becomes complete' (often through marriage); the warrior companion becomes a king or leader of some kind; the comic companion takes centre stage, even if briefly; and the old man with a stick returns from death to wrap up the core vacuum that he introduced us to in the first place and has reminded us of all along.

So in *The Lord of the Rings*, Frodo discovers a new inner peace and journeys to Valinor, Arwen marries Aragorn and Eowyn marries Faramir, Aragorn becomes king, Sam becomes Mayor of Michel Delving and takes over after Frodo leaves, and Gandalf the Grey returns as Gandalf the White and sees everything through to victory. In a classic fantasy novel of this kind it's relatively easy to see these separate strands, but they are also almost as clear in a modern realistic novel like *To Kill a Mockingbird*: Scout becomes complete (through her revelations at the end); Boo (as the 'warrior figure') is redeemed; Dill plays his key role in the plot; and Atticus, the old man with the stick (or rifle) sees out the theme of social justice, suggesting hope at the end.

In Tragedies - in Shakespearian dramas, for example - the inner character vacuums are often glimpsed by us through the protagonist's soliloquys, as we have seen. But the whole tragedy is that the expected vacuum is left largely unfilled: Macbeth's expectations that he should be king of Scotland go awry; Lear's expectations that he can unmock his kingdom, divide it up and still have a good life are undone; Othello's desire for a good marriage are undermined by Iago's subterfuge. And, beyond Shakespeare, Anakin Skywalker's craving for justice and order are betrayed by his master, the Emperor.

In Ironies, the vacuums are unexpected and then made worse - sudden death, unwanted changes of identity, mysteries which are solved in shocking ways. In *Great Expectations*, for example, Pip had no idea at first that he might want to be a gentleman, but this desire is sparked in him and then betrayed; in *An Inspector Calls*, the pleasant family gathering is unexpectedly destroyed layer by amplified layer by the visit from the Inspector and even the hope that order can be restored is swept aside by the impact of the play's ending.

By the time we get to Comedy, the pattern is predictable from the above: if Epics have expected vacuums which are filled in various ways, Tragedies have expected vacuums which are left unfilled, and Ironies have unexpected vacuums made worse, then Comedies as the last of the broad genre types should have unexpected vacuums filled in unexpected ways. And this is what we find: a joke is simply the creation of an unexpected vacuum and its filling in a surprising way.

Punchlines are always surprising, or should be.

Whether you want to write an Epic saga, a dark historical Tragedy, a modern psychological Irony or a lighthearted romantic Comedy, keep in mind the patterns suggested here. They will act to keep your work 'on the rails' so that readers are not left puzzled, disappointed or confused.

This table might help keep it clear for you. (A fuller table exists in the Appendix at the end of this book.)

GENRE	VACUUMS	OUTCOMES
Epic	Expected	Filled in traditional ways
Tragedy	Expected	Unfulfilled
Irony	Unexpected	Worsened
Comedy	Unexpected	Filled in unexpected ways

Vacuums and Emotional Commitment

There are people. And there are vacuums. It can even be argued that people are made out of vacuums. 'Vacuum' here is another word for need or desire, with the added implication that a vacuum generates an actual pulling force which is what brings a person into contact with whatever is needed.

Vacuums can be of different sizes or intensities.

A non-existent vacuum generates no pulling force. To bring two or more things together, a vacuum must be created between them. Smaller vacuums - vacuums to do with a loss of comforts or luxuries - are less powerful and generate only a mild pulling force. Larger vacuums - vacuums to do with deeper and more commonly desired things - are more powerful and generate a stronger force. The largest vacuums of all, to do with health, security, life and death, have the strongest pull of all.

Lesser vacuums can be linked to larger vacuums make them stronger and more effective. As these interlinked vacuums drag reader attention along from sentence to sentence, page to page, chapter to chapter, act to act, emotion is generated.

The emotional fulfilment of a piece of fiction is determined by the promise of the size and amount of vacuums filled.

The moments we treasure in reading fiction are moments of fulfilment.

Gandalf's return in *The Lord of the Rings*; the destruction of the Death Star in *Star Wars a New Hope*; George Bailey's homecoming in *It's a Wonderful Life*; Scout's revelations in *To Kill a Mockingbird* - all of these and thousands more are moments of warmth and triumph when a vacuum which the author has created has been successfully filled.

Macbeth's last moment of courage and his death; Hamlet's noble demise; the uncertainty over Pip's future at the end of *Great Expectations*; the chilling ending of *An Inspector Calls* - all these are masterfully crafted vacuums which are then purposely *not* filled by the author, leaving the reader in a cold unknown.

On the way, the author has caused the 'magnetic' phenomenon of emotion to occur.

Is there a finite supply of emotion in any given story? That would be like saying that there is a finite number of vacuums in any given work.

Of course there isn't. There are an almost infinite number of potential vacuums, large or small, in any given set of characters and in any plot, whatever its genre. It may take a little skill to create them, but vacuums are everywhere and of every kind.

Having grasped the 'physics of fiction' in this way, how do you start implementing these principles in your own work?

Part Two:

The Five Stage Fiction Model

Chapter Thirteen:
Developing Fiction That Really Works

You have the broad idea now: you can appreciate the principles behind vacuum-power and you have had some guidance as to how it all might work to get more readers for your own fiction than you have ever imagined, retain them and make them happier than they ever dreamed of.

You've seen a few examples of how this has worked for others. But how can you actually make it work for you and your work?

This section walks you through setting up a vacuum-powered piece of fiction, beginning with you and the actions that you can implement straight away to get your work functioning properly, then moving on to extend your thinking into realms you've probably never considered. By the time you have finished, you should have a work model designed to generate huge reader satisfaction. For a step-by-step highly practical approach, you can also consult the companion volume to this book, *How Stories Really Work - A Practical Manual to Transform Your Fiction,* and if you need more help, there's the twelve-week e-course *How to Write Stories That Work - and Get Them Published!* both available through Clarendon House Publications.

The process of building a successful work of fiction can be reduced to a series of five stages.

Stage 1

Stage 1 is You, as a writer.

Successful fiction isn't created by simply pushing ideas at the reader - that is usually counter-productive. Most stories at least attempt to fill some kind of vacuum for readers, or they would not persist as stories. A few go further and become great works of literature.

But the source of all stories, at least as they appear to us, is a writer. What does that writer believe? What personal vacuums motivate him or her? Are they positive, negative, internal, external, or a mixture of all? Which vacuums will he or she select to drive the story?

90% of fiction will fail to even get written, let alone published, if the writer doesn't have an appropriate motivation to do so. What do *you* believe? Why must *your* story be written?

Is this going to be an uplifting story in which vacuums are filled? Or a disturbing or introverting story in which vacuums are left open or empty?

Which engine are you going to choose to drive your fiction?

A common practice in literary criticism is to try to trace back the elements of a story to its author's psychology. While it's true that every human being has vacuums of his or her own, this type of analysis misses out on the step of selection: which vacuums will the author *choose* to use, personal or otherwise, in the construction of a story? It also misses the basic fact that most vacuums have interconnections far beyond the comprehension of any single author or reader.

That's why stories can have so much meaning; that's why there are whole libraries devoted to the significances to be found in Shakespeare; that's why the map of significance has no edges and can never have any. Readers bring their own vacuums and interconnections to any work of fiction, adding in further dimensions and layers of sense and connotations.

You as a writer are just as dwarfed by all this as any reader. You should work hard to increase the significance of your fiction, but at the end of your work the web of inter-relationships will be outside your grasp just as it is outside any one person's grasp.

Stage 1 is the internal world of the author.

Selecting out from his or her experience and imagination the core vacuums for a work of fiction gives us Stage 2.

Putting together character, linear and mystery vacuums to effectively 'sell' those core vacuums to readers is Stage 3.

Stage 4 consists of the bridging of the story to its particular target audience.

Stage 5 is the word and sentence level use of vacuums to grip and hold attention on every page.

In your work, you must have some kind of idea of what you are offering to the public, even if you are still in the planning stage. You should at least have a notion of whether you have written or want to write a Comedy or an Epic, or a Tragedy or an Irony.

Perhaps you want your epic fantasy to rival Tolkien's or George R. R. Martin's and have some idea of the sense of wonder you want to leave readers with.

Maybe you are imagining a romantic novel which you would like to emotionally grip readers while also stretching the boundaries of the genre.

Possibly you have in mind a grand tragedy with the fall of a great figure prompting introspection in a range of readers.

Or you might have a collection of short horror stories in mind, designed to produce shock and a sense of nightmare.

In each case, large or small, the engine that drives the story will be its *core vacuum*. But your first task as a writer is to determine which core vacuum you are going to use.

If you are burning to write a particular story or set of stories, and already have a clear idea of what you are going to write, then you will still benefit from clarifying what these core vacuums will be. That's Stage 2.

Stage 2

When you first established your work, or first made plans to do so, you probably had an idea of what your main 'message' would be. Stage 2, though, requires that you go 'back to the drawing board' to some degree - but in an exciting and very positive way. Stage 2 is the beginning of escalating your work into a higher realm of meaning and satisfaction.

If you have an existing piece of fiction, or an idea for one, you need to list what you think its core vacuums are. What is it about?

The Lord of the Rings' core vacuum is the struggle between the forces of life and death. It's an Epic because the forces of Life win, though not without some loss.

Macbeth's core vacuum is the struggle between the protagonist's conscience and temptation. It's a Tragedy because he loses.

Great Expectations is driven by the core vacuum of Pip's desire for satisfaction and love. It's an Irony because it's not at all clear at the end of the novel that this vacuum is filled.

Pride and Prejudice has at its heart the need for romantic fulfilment, which comes with the social benefits of marriage in this case, as this is a Romance, fitting into the genre of Comedy. The union of Elizabeth and Darcy fills the core vacuum.

All the other techniques of the stories above are designed to attract and hold enough readers or audience so that they 'buy' the core ideas.

Take your existing fiction or idea and examine it closely. What are its core vacuums? Then ask, how could those core vacuums be expanded into something bigger, deeper, better, wider, more powerful or more valuable?

Your key question is:

'How can I take my existing core vacuums and *dramatically add meaning* to them?'

Look at the vacuums that your work already seeks to fill. Are there *bigger* vacuums associated with those? Are there *connected* vacuums? Are there areas of need which, with some work and adjustments, you could tap into?

For example, C. S. Lewis's story *The Lion, the Witch and the Wardrobe* could have been a simple chase story, good versus evil, with some fighting and so on. But, by adding in layers of meaning, by creating a religious allegory, or simply by tapping into basic vacuums to do with life, death and morality, Lewis created a long-lasting children's classic.

The entire *Star Wars* saga could have been a 'Western in space', a shoot-out between two-dimensional good guys and shallow, typical bad guys, like many of its imitators. What gave it depth and resonance was the basic vacuums that were tapped into through mentions of the cosmic 'Force', the character vacuums associated with Luke's father, and so on. *Star Wars* continues to grow today not because it was a yarn about heroes and villains, but because it connected with something deeper.

Without working on Stage 2, your work as a writer may be wasted by being too superficial. Linear, mystery and moral vacuums, working with character vacuums, can still create good stories on their own - but core vacuums magnify their power and give it meaning. It's a question of connecting vacuums together. This can be more clearly seen if we take another look at the categories of vacuums outlined earlier.

The Protagonist's Journey

Firstly, let's look at the Protagonist's Journey from the reader's point of view, as per the following diagram. The reader normally lives in a world where he or she only experiences mild discomforts or inconveniences as vacuums - things missing in life. Of course, worse things happen to readers as human beings from time to time, but the 'average reader' at any given moment will have universal vacuums of some sort in play in life.

A protagonist, as we have seen, has certain common gaps or absences or mysteries in existence, usually including missing parents, but as far as the plot is concerned should start off at the level of the second circle from the left, sharing a reality with the reader, discomfited and unhappy in some way without really being distinctly threatened. There is an overlap, then, in the worlds of the reader and the protagonist - something we'll develop in Stage 4 - beginning with the lighter universal vacuums common to both in degree; this then moves from left to right as the plot vacuums get larger and larger, ending with the core vacuum at the extreme right. This gives you the direction of the story from beginning to conclusion. If you successfully fill the core vacuum at the end, you have created an Epic or Comedy; if you leave it intentionally empty, you have created a Tragedy or an Irony.

Looking at the diagram shows us where the story is getting its power from.

All fiction gains power and meaning from its core vacuums.

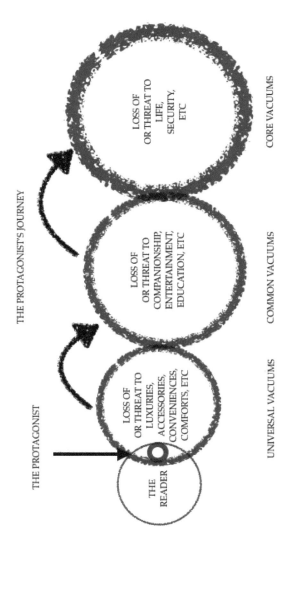

Imagine the core vacuum as the nuclear reactor, the electric generator, the beating heart of your story. From it pulse the megawatts of energy that give your story energy and meaning. Craft a good core vacuum and the rest of the story more or less writes itself. Its vacuum power will grab and grip reader attention and pull the reader along through the lesser vacuums that in the end build up to it.

How do core vacuums interact with the other vacuums in a story? As stated earlier, all other vacuums exist to grab and hold reader attention with the intention of 'selling' the core vacuum to the reader, i.e. getting the reader to emotionally commit to it. The more you can get the linear, mystery, moral and character vacuums to relate to the core vacuum, the better your story will be.

What traditional advice about writing calls the 'climax' of any piece of fiction has to do with one such interrelationship.

The collision between the protagonist's character vacuums and the core vacuum is the climax of a tale.

Frodo's desperation to serve the cause of Good clashes at the heart of Sauron's realm with the Dark Lord's destructive centre that threatens all of Middle Earth; Frodo is overwhelmed by the power of the Ring and succumbs to the temptation of power, almost transforming the whole tale into an Irony - it is only the 'fateful' intervention of Gollum that saves the world. Frodo rediscovers himself, emerging from under the shadow of the Ring, but has such large vacuums (wounds, dark memories) that he can only really be fully healed by journeying to Valinor.

Luke Skywalker's search for the goodness in his father on board the second Death Star impacts with the Emperor's evil plan to dominate the galaxy; Luke is almost killed by the Emperor when he cannot be turned to the Dark Side, again bringing the story to the verge of an Irony - only his father's last minute intervention and sacrifice changes things. Luke is saved and goes on to become a full Jedi.

Captain America's search for the last vestiges of his lost era run into the Winter Soldier's defiance and support of the plan to destroy the freedom of the world; Rogers is almost killed by his former friend Bucky, but in the end Bucky saves him by dragging his body ashore. Rogers recovers to become leader of the Avengers.

Macbeth's attempt to fulfil his own character vacuum of kingly ambition meets the witches' knowledge of events that work against him; Macbeth is robbed one by one of his hopes, and fails. As this is a Tragedy, he is not saved but perishes.

In *Great Expectations* Pip's desire to reach a status where Estella will take him seriously encounters the full force of the law as it seeks to eliminate criminality; Pip succumbs to illness and loses everything. As this is an Irony, it is highly doubtful whether he regains anything at the end.

Character vacuum meets core vacuum: in Epics and Comedies, the protagonist is almost lost, but survives through some kind of miraculous intervention. In Tragedies and Ironies, nothing intervenes and the protagonist is overwhelmed.

Linear, mystery and moral vacuums have served their purpose at this point. They exist to get your reader to the point where the protagonist makes a choice right at the heart of the story: will he act to fill the core vacuum or not?

In Forster's *A Passage to India*, Adela Quested's inner needs overlap with the needs of the entire community. She flounders and fails, but a deeper meaning is revealed, again depending on how the last part of the Ironic novel is read.

But the fact remains that, no matter what successful story is examined, no matter the genre, the climax is the coming together of the character's innermost desires with the story world's uppermost needs.

This is the progression we have seen in the examples that we have examined, ranging from Shakespeare to contemporary films. This is the progression that your leading character needs to make in order to secure the most reader empathy and hold the attention in the story.

How deep and meaningful do you want to make your fulfilling chapters at the end of the tale? Do you want your characters to simply survive or win a battle, thus fulfilling the classic 'What happens next?' linear vacuum of the plot? Do you want the mysteries resolved and everything clarified, thus fulfilling the 'What is going on?' mystery vacuums of the story? This will satisfy readers and produce a reasonably successful work of fiction.

But if you want to create a long-lasting masterpiece, or at least a more powerful work which stands the test of time and is read again and again, you need to include as much meaning as possible in your core vacuums: not only does the protagonist need to survive, he or she needs to discover the meaning of that life; not only does a world have to be saved, it has to be saved for a purpose or in such a way that resonates with significance.

To be a truly successful author, you need to fulfil core vacuums until they overflow with fulfilment and resonate with meaning.

Per the diagrams above, through your protagonist you're leading a reader into a terrible zone of vacuums where life or sanity or both can be threatened. If you don't fulfil that expectation well, all your work can be wasted or not quite ring true.

But if you do fulfil it with meaning, your work will become a classic.

The idea of Stage 2 is to have a powerful, lingering effect on a reader. This comes from having core vacuums which resonate so deeply that they tap into universal themes: love, peace, life and death, what it means to be alive and so forth.

C. S. Lewis's children's fiction is one example. He creates a fantasy world, but that fantasy world intersects with the world in which we live. We discover, quite unexpectedly, that the back of an old wardrobe is a door into another world. This intersects with something every child feels - the sense of surprise and the encounter with the unexpected. Lewis then connects it with a whole different level of experience and gives readers more than they expected.

Chapter Fourteen:
Boosting Your Existing Fiction

Right now, you may have a work of fiction which you currently offer or want to offer to the public, with no changes, tweaks, modifications or adaptations of any kind. Perhaps you aren't writing enough, and perhaps you have already realised that various changes need to be made to your work and the way you operate. But let's begin by taking what you already have, no matter what shape it is in.

How can you apply vacuum power to this existing picture?

Has vacuum power already been at work in your work? If what we have been talking about is in any way true, then yes, the thing that has been keeping your work afloat in terms of meaning, character motivation and reader relations has been vacuum power, whether you recognised it as such or not. Characters and plots have been driven by something, however unsatisfactory, and readers have been attracted and driven by something, even if it hasn't been as strong as you would wish.

How do you work out what those already existing vacuums are?

Isolating Character Vacuums

Firstly, take the work you have written and break it down as follows:

Look for the *most obvious* character vacuum.

This is the thing that your current protagonist most lacks or feels is missing. This is what gives your protagonist the most attractive power in the whole work. Even if that power is still weaker than you would like, this is the item which you should immediately develop in any way you can. If it is already attracting reader attention, it is capable of attracting more. So your first action should be *to boost the already-existing character vacuum in your protagonist.*

Perhaps your hero is missing a limb or (more likely) lacks a stable family background. Magnify this. Make his or her weakness greater, either by hinting at basic vacuums - threats to life itself - or at common vacuums - loss of companionship or opportunities.

187

It's quite possible, though, that the most attractive thing in your existing work isn't your protagonist at all. It should be, but then you have only just had 'protagonist' defined in these terms in this book as *the point in a story which attracts most of the reader's attention with vacuums*. Perhaps there's a lesser character that you've constructed with more vacuums and you were wondering why that figure seemed attractive in his or her own right. Now you know. You have a choice: either shift the vacuum intensity over to your original protagonist by giving him or her more vacuums, or transfer the 'protagonist-ship' over to the other character. Writers who do this sometimes give their stories a whole new lease of life: they've been trying to tell the story from the viewpoint of the wrong character! Move a more attractive character into the central position and the story explodes into life.

Work this over until you have created as many character vacuums as seem appropriate. Too many, and the character starts to become a comedy construct: exaggerated losses can act to prompt laughter, like the knight in *Monty Python and the Holy Grail* who keeps acting defiantly despite the loss of all his limbs. You need to be the judge of which character vacuums will work in the context of your story - but don't be afraid to magnify those needs, losses, cravings, desires.

Then take the next most likely character vacuum and promote that, and so on. This won't get your fiction into the stellar levels that you're dreaming about, but it will instantly boost the energy of your fiction while you work on the much more powerful measures that are coming up.

Now look over the story for the other character archetypes that we have described: the comic companion who brings temporary relief? The female companion who personifies a vacuum? The warrior companion who appears duplicitous at first? And who is performing the role of the old man with the stick?

If they are not present, insert them. A couple of examples of this may help you to see what happens when you do.

Back in the 1960s, in the Marvel comic *Daredevil*, young Matt Murdock gained super-enhanced senses including a 'radar sense' which enabled him to see all around him, though blinded after an accident with a truck carrying radio-active chemicals. For two decades, Daredevil did well as a Marvel character with his own comic book series. Then, in the 1980s, comic book artist and writer Frank Miller took charge of the character and re-structured his 'origin story', giving him a stern mentor figure who trained the fledgeling hero in the use of his powers. This old man carried a staff and was named Stick. He pointed out deeper lackings in Murdock's personality and a larger external core vacuum for the hero. *Daredevil* as a series went into best-seller mode as readers, consciously or not, picked up on all of these archetypal additives.

Still in the superhero world, Richard Donner's classic film *Superman* expanded the role of its protagonist's father, a little-seen character from the comics called Jor-El, into a standard 'old man with a stick' character. Jor-El's 'stick' was the green crystal seen in the film which his son used to create the crystalline Fortress of Solitude and communicate with his father. The film went on to huge success and is still considered a model for superhero movies to this day.

In the world of television, consider the long-running BBC science fiction series *Doctor Who*. This began in 1963 with character archetypes in place - standard hero protagonist Ian Chesterton accompanied by female companion Barbara Wright discover that the mysterious Susan Freeman is actually the grand-daughter of a time travelling alien called 'the Doctor', who initially was very much the 'old man with a stick' mentor figure. Later, writers even gave him a 'stick', a 'sonic screwdriver' with a range of functions so vast that it became his magic wand. As the series went on, the Doctor through his various incarnations came to cover some of the other character archetype functions himself, including comic companion and warrior king, but he usually reverted to the old man mentor type. It goes without saying that the series continues to thrive in various media even after five decades. Note also that for the first few years the television audience had no idea who the character was or where he came from - a real mystery vacuum. Even today, the Doctor's true name remains unknown.

So look for these archetypes and develop them, giving each his or her appropriate character vacuums to ensure that as a constructed person they are attractive to readers.

Isolating Plot Vacuums

Then take your plot, whatever shape it is in. By far the majority of plots, in order to be plots at all, as we have seen, have to contain at least one linear vacuum, the question 'What happens next?' being a universal requirement of story-telling. But the ramblings of a writer's imagination don't always fulfil this requirement.

Take what you have and create suspense in some way by inserting vacuums: what exactly *will* happen next? Is there a race, chase or hunt sequence where it is not immediately obvious who will win? Work over your existing tale and pump into it as many linear vacuums as you can. You will find your plot coming to life with each unknown outcome you insert.

If you can relate the linear vacuum to character vacuums, all the better. The children's race to find Aslan in *The Lion, the Witch and the Wardrobe* is a powerful linear vacuum which drives the whole plot, but it is made more effective because it is also linked to their character vacuum desires to see their brother again; Luke Skywalker's final run on the Death Star in *Star Wars: A New Hope* is a gripping linear vacuum which closely relates to his maturation as a young Jedi, filling his own character vacuum.

Mystery vacuums are part of this. What is really going on in your story? Is there some kind of sub-text, or is what readers see all that they get? Are your constructed characters just going through the motions created by linear vacuums, or are they also internally driven by a desire to find the answer to a puzzle? Create mysteries and pump them into your story.

J. K. Rowling's *Harry Potter* series is virtually powered by mystery vacuums alone: page after page is turned, as the small group of Hogwarts students desperately seeks the solution to a series of intriguing unknowns, most of them linked to Harry's character vacuum, his loss of his parents. All detective stories are built around at least one mystery, usually several. Again, link these mysteries to the characters and your story gains depth and gravity. What is motivating your protagonist? Is he or she simply on a journey somewhere? Or is there also a desperate quest to find an answer to a mystery?

The combination of added linear vacuums and fascinating mystery vacuums, mixed with a series of gripping character vacuums, gives you the recipe for totally transforming your work.

Looking for Fulfilment

You should answer the following questions based on your top five favourite pieces of fiction of all time, books or films or plays.

Ask yourself:

• What was the need which drove you to read that book or see that play or film?

• What did you expect when you did?

• How would you rate the performance of the work in bringing you some kind of fulfilment?

The more specific you can be, the more useful your answers will be.

For example, you might say that you first were attracted to *The Lord of the Rings* by the mention of quests and elves and a created fictional world on a grand scale. Your expectations might have been that you would be drawn into a world which would be both similar to our own but sufficiently different to be intriguing. How would you rate *The Lord of the Rings* in terms of fulfilment? Did it live up to its original promise? Did it surpass your expectations?

Answer the same questions for your other four favourite works of fiction.

Now, having accumulated some answers, can you replicate those kinds of things in your work? Any data which you can use to help to fulfil that purpose in your fiction is worth gold to you.

What are the needs which might drive readers to your epic fantasy or your romantic novel or your grand tragedy or your collection of short horror stories? What are readers expecting when they pick up or see a work of fiction by you? What kinds of people are they? Are there patterns there? And how do you think they would rate your ability to fulfil their initial expectations?

Are you confident that you can *exceed* those expectations?

Stage Three, then, boosts the power of your work immediately. But we still have Stages Four and Five to come. These stages, as you will see, will form a powerful channel out into the world which will widen into a super-highway for new readers if used correctly.

Stage 4

Your task in Stage 4 is to take the character and plot vacuums that you have already developed and *make them more real to your target audience.*

Look for the area from which most of your readers have come or from where you would like them to come.

This could be a particular gender - in which case you should concentrate your attention on that gender - or it could be an age group - e.g. the teen market. Look for common denominators among these readers. Do they all have a similar cultural background? What else are they likely to have read or seen? All of these things, and any other clues you can glean from your existing knowledge, give you an indication of the vacuums that might be put to work in your fiction.

The *Harry Potter* series struck at the children's market with a combination of powerful vacuums: the need for a simple vocabulary adventure story featuring children of a particular age group combined with a desire for schooling to be magical, literally. It was interesting to observe that a large part of the market for Harry Potter when he first appeared was those children who struggled to get interested in reading as a whole. They wanted to be interested, they just didn't know how to start and were striking barriers when they attempted it. J. K. Rowling's material - a school environment filled with magic - both began from a base with which those children had some familiarity while embellishing it with imaginative ideas. Her unchallenging writing style and basic vocabulary presented fewer barriers. And with each successive book, the Potter phenomenon grew with loyal readers desperate for the next release.

The *Twilight* series similarly tapped into the teenage market with its sense of isolation and hormonal flows to create a best-selling love story about vampires. The feelings exhibited by the main characters were hardly supernatural - the readers could relate.

Could you replicate this in some way in your own fiction? Not by writing stories about learning magic at school or vampire love (there are already many who have tried to do that) but by taking something very familiar to your age group or gender of readers and injecting it with new life and energy?

This takes minimal effort and may require no real modification of your writing.

What you are doing in Stage 4 is working on *universal vacuums*, making them fit the likely universal vacuums of your particular public.

Move the initial gaps, holes, needs, desires and so on upwards or outwards from basic and common vacuums to do with life, death health, loss of friends or missed opportunities into the slightly lighter realm of universal vacuums - curtailed time, threats to comforts, frustrations about changes.

Why does this work?

The further up and out vacuums go, the more universal they become.

For example, in *Star Wars: A New Hope* we meet Luke Skywalker not in an outer space battle with his nemesis, but on a farm, beleaguered by chores given to him by his grumpy uncle in the same way that many teenagers feel constrained by adults around them. We meet Frodo Baggins in *The Lord of the Rings* not in some outlying part of Wilderland fighting a dragon but in the recognisable domestic setting of the Shire, bothered by relatives. We encounter Scout, protagonist of *To Kill a Mockingbird*, not in the dramatic courtroom of later scenes but in her own garden, confronted by the challenges of a first day at school. Successful authors take pains, whether they are conscious of it or not, to build a firm bridge between us and the constructed characters that they are introducing to us: their vacuums must be our vacuums, at least in the beginning.

Taking what you've isolated about your target market, you can take this a stage further. What kind of additional or universal vacuums have your readers experienced? Unhappiness at school? Frustration in a relationship? Unwanted change of location? The teenage market is so huge and alive for fiction mainly because it possesses so much scope for vacuums of this kind: the parameters of a teenager's life are established by adults, by definition, which leads to relatively mild frustrations and constraints of all kinds.

Similarly, if you are writing or planning to write a romantic comedy aimed at young or middle-aged women, the question to ask to build your bridging vacuums is what kind of light but universal vacuums do these women experience? Disappointment in long-term relationships? Mild health issues? Concerns about appearance? *Bridget Jones Diary* became an international bestseller by tapping into those kinds of things.

Start with the universally recognisable vacuums and you will haul in a large catch of readers.

How Vacuums Fit Together

You will have seen that by now in any successful work of fiction you have core vacuums, hidden by mystery vacuums, punctuated by moral vacuums, surrounded by linear vacuums and encompassed by character vacuums. Character vacuums draw the reader in; linear vacuums drive the reader on; moral vacuums engage the reader's sense of ethics; mystery vacuums grip the reader's attention. And core vacuums deliver the fulfilling moment (or purposely unfulfilling moment in Tragedies and Ironies) at the end.

For example, in *To Kill a Mockingbird* we are drawn in by the way Scout and the other children are portrayed, their character vacuums mainly being composed of an endearing and common child's innocence and ignorance of the world. Then we are gripped by the mystery vacuums surrounding Boo Radley before being driven by the increasingly tense linear vacuum of the unfolding courtroom testimony. Finally, the powerful message of the novel is delivered through the core vacuum when the villain of the story, Bob Ewell, attacks and attempts to kill the children. He fails and Scout's revelation at the end of the novel fulfils us.

In *It's a Wonderful Life*, the physical and emotional losses of protagonist George Bailey make him attractive to us before we are moved forward by the linear vacuum of his life story and enthralled by the mystery of the angel Clarence's appearance and his alteration of reality. Then we are compelled by the core vacuum as George's threatened arrest and suicide are averted, resulting in our moment of Christmas fulfilment.

In *Pride and Prejudice*, Elizabeth Bennett's mildly ironic view of life captivates us enough so that the linear vacuum of her family's developing connections with the nobility are able to carry us forward while we are intrigued by the mysteries presented by Wickham. Eventually we are engaged enough to be gripped by the core vacuum as family ruin is threatened and then avoided in the final chapters, with the fulfilling marriage of Elizabeth to Mr. Darcy crowning the ending.

Stage 4 vacuums throw a wide net and then the vacuum-powered machine of a successful work of fiction comes into play to produce the resulting fulfilment for the reader.

What about Stage 5?

Chapter Fifteen:
The Vacuum Interface

Almost everything that people have said about literature through the ages fits into Stage 5.

That's because Stage 5 is the actual 'interface' between the written work and the reader. This is where the result of all the structuring and conceptualising and formatting that has been accomplished in the other stages lies in the form of an open page before another person, who then reads it.

As we have seen, vacuums are an incredibly useful tool or analogy to help you develop your ideas as a writer, build character constructs that actually grip and attract reader attention, as well as assisting you in creating plots which really drive the reader through the text. But there is yet another dimension to them which can help you broaden your readership too.

Vacuums also operate at page and sentence level.

The startling truth is that vacuum power doesn't only apply to character, plot or structure - it applies to sentence-level and even word-level writing.

Vacuums used subtly and consistently can create, consciously or otherwise, precise structures and recurring patterns at sentence level.

Vacuums in Charles Dickens' 'The Signalman'

We can examine this more closely by looking at a short story by Charles Dickens in some detail. Examining a text in close detail like this reveals what techniques a master author uses to engage and manipulate a reader's attention.

It's not for nothing that Dickens is perhaps the most famous of all English novelists. His novels are notable not only for their humour and treatment of social problems of his time, including the troubles faced by the poor in the newly expanding cities of Victorian England, and the corruption and inefficiency of the legal system, but also for their richness of style and their apparently effortless ability to engage the reader. *Great Expectations* (1860–61) in particular is a triumph of the Irony genre, and that novel, as we have seen, is a study in the expert use of vacuum power, whether Dickens himself would have used the term or not.

Dickens lived well before the age of movies or television, yet his stories are very visual and dramatic, partly because he wrote them in instalments for magazines (which operate, like any kind of serialised story, on the 'cliffhanger' of a linear vacuum - 'What happens next?') His characters and their settings, especially London, are well described, linger in our imaginations and come to life on the page - and there are specific reasons why.

'The Signalman', a short story which Dickens wrote for a journal he was producing, called *All the Year Round*, first appeared in 1866, when Britain was undergoing huge changes and was in the middle of what we now call the Industrial Revolution. Railways had recently been invented and had spread across the countryside like spiders' webs; there was a glamour and a mystery about the sheer power of steam locomotives as they thundered down the railway lines which were now criss-crossing the once-peaceful countryside. It would have been as though flying buses appeared above our towns today - new modes of transport promised unknown developments in society, and prompted new thoughts and images.

'The Signalman' is also a ghost story, and the Victorians loved ghost stories - but this was a time when new sciences like psychoanalysis were beginning to probe the unconscious dreams and nightmares of people. Many were questioning whether traditional forms of belief like Christianity were true or how far the precepts really extended into the vastness of the rapidly unfolding universe or the darkness of our own minds. Just what was the truth about the universe and human souls? Dickens capitalises on all this from the very first line of the story:

'Halloa! Below there!'

When he heard a voice thus calling to him, he was standing at the door of his box, with a flag in his hand, furled round its short pole. One would have thought, considering the nature of the ground, that he could not have doubted from what quarter the voice came; but instead of looking up to where I stood on the top of the steep cutting nearly over his head, he turned himself about, and looked down the Line. There was something remarkable in his manner of doing so, though I could not have said for my life what. But I know it was remarkable enough to attract my notice, even though his figure was foreshortened and shadowed, down in the deep trench, and mine was high above him, so steeped in the glow of an angry sunset, that I had shaded my eyes with my hand before I saw him at all.

'Halloa! Below!'

We start in a void: there is none of the traditional 'scene-setting' common to stories. We have to interpret a kind of code to get even a vague idea of where we are: the 'door of his box', the 'flag in his hand, furled round its short pole', and then a few words later 'the steep cutting'. The author doesn't pause to carefully explain the setting, but just plunges us into the vacuum and expects us to put the scene together on our own. This isn't unintentional - it's part of the disorientation which Dickens creates to prompt a slight 'fictive vertigo' in the reader. This is a telltale Irony technique. He magnifies it soon afterwards with this passage:

He looked up at me without replying, and I looked down at him without pressing him too soon with a repetition of my idle question. Just then there came a vague vibration in the earth and air, quickly changing into a violent pulsation, and an oncoming rush that caused me to start back, as though it had force to draw me down.

What is happening here? Some kind of unknown, 'vague' but 'violent pulsation' enters the scene in an 'oncoming rush' which prompts the narrator to 'start back' afraid that he will be drawn down. The result? Fictive vertigo increased through a combination of linear ('What will happen next?') and mystery ('What is going on?') vacuums. It's not until the next sentence that the source of this strangeness is explained, in a single sentence which restores some stability and order to things:

When such vapour as rose to my height from this rapid train had passed me, and was skimming away over the landscape, I looked down again, and saw him refurling the flag he had shown while the train went by.

But Dickens is a master of rhythm. Before we can gain any comfort or even get our bearings, he describes the narrator's descent into the railway cutting in terms designed to unsettle us with further vacuums:

> The cutting was extremely deep, and unusually precipitate. It was made through a clammy stone, that became oozier and wetter as I went down. For these reasons, I found the way long enough to give me time to recall a singular air of reluctance or compulsion with which he had pointed out the path.

The use of words is precise: 'extremely deep', 'unusually precipitate', 'clammy', 'oozier and 'wetter' as the narrator goes 'down'. The way is long enough to give him time to recall the 'singular air of reluctance or compulsion' with which the signalman had pointed out the path. It's also long enough for Dickens to be able to insert that sentence, amplifying our sense of unease by adding vacuum after vacuum through words alone.

Dickens takes pains to describe the exact manner in which the signalman is waiting for the narrator: 'He had his left hand at his chin, and that left elbow rested on his right hand, crossed over his breast. His attitude was one of such expectation and watchfulness that I stopped a moment, wondering at it.' What is this man thinking? Why point out these details to us except to undermine any certainties we might be trying to establish? Thus the mystery vacuums are increased.

Then we are hit over the space of only a few lines by a disproportionate number of gloomy adjectives, nouns and verbs: 'dark', 'sallow', 'heavy', 'solitary', 'dismal', 'dripping-wet', 'jagged', 'crooked', 'dungeon', 'terminating', 'gloomy', 'gloomier', 'black', 'massive', 'barbarous', 'depressing', 'forbidding', 'earthy', 'deadly', 'cold', 'rushed', 'struck' and 'chill'. Dickens the master author uses words like bullets. The cumulative effect is to make the narrator feel 'as if I had left the natural world.' And so, to a lesser but nevertheless marked degree, do we. Natural expectations and comfortable settings have been shot down.

This is again using words as vacuum-generators. They stack up, adding to our sense of something missing, a gap, a darkness, embodied in the tunnel itself.

The narrator's attempt to strike up a 'normal' conversation fails at first: 'To such purpose I spoke to him; but I am far from sure of the terms I used; for, besides that I am not happy in opening any conversation, there was something in the man that daunted me.' And by now the narrator has been so bombarded by discomfiting sensations and responses that a 'monstrous thought' comes into his mind that 'as I perused the fixed eyes and the saturnine face, that this was a spirit, not a man. I have speculated since, whether there may have been infection in his mind.'

The unsettling vacuums created by the precise use of language has the effect of stirring deeper, basic vacuums - we are on the edge of sanity itself. A series of rapid-fire questions and answers dispel these forebodings, but nervously:

In my turn, I stepped back. But in making the action, I detected in his eyes some latent fear of me. This put the monstrous thought to flight.

'You look at me,' I said, forcing a smile, 'as if you had a dread of me.'

'I was doubtful,' he returned, 'whether I had seen you before.'

'Where?'

He pointed to the red light he had looked at.

'There?' I said.

Intently watchful of me, he replied (but without sound), 'Yes.'

'My good fellow, what should I do there? However, be that as it may, I never was there, you may swear.'

'I think I may,' he rejoined. 'Yes; I am sure I may.'

What follows is a nerve-steadying couple of paragraphs of ordinariness: the signalman describes his life in the signal-box in a manner that we might expect. His life, in fact, has for the most part 'shaped itself into that form, and he had grown used to it.' In the room there are the ordinary things one might expect to find in a signal-box: a fire, a desk for an official book, a telegraphic instrument with its dial, face, and needles, and a little bell. The narrator observes the signalman 'to be remarkably exact and vigilant, breaking off his discourse at a syllable, and remaining silent until what he had to do was done' and concludes that 'I should have set this man down as one of the safest of men to be employed in that capacity' except for one thing.

Dickens, settling us down with these comforting associations, which serve to partly fill the vacuums he has laboured to create, now explodes them. The 'one thing' that deeply concerns the narrator about the signalman is that

> while he was speaking to me he twice broke off with a fallen colour, turned his face towards the little bell when it did NOT ring, opened the door of the hut (which was kept shut to exclude the unhealthy damp), and looked out towards the red light near the mouth of the tunnel. On both of those occasions, he came back to the fire with the inexplicable air upon him which I had remarked, without being able to define, when we were so far asunder.

The signalman's confession that he is 'troubled' would lead, in the hands of a lesser author, to an immediate unfolding of the mysteries which have been brewed for us so far. But Dickens is a master author, and so intrudes a further delay by having the narrator return to his inn for one night, promising to return the next day. There is no need for this overnight delay - the signalman could just have easily told the narrator the whole story then and there. But Dickens knows that adding time into the story - extending the linear vacuum of 'What happens next?' and magnifying the mystery vacuum of 'What is going on?' - at this point serves to increase the suspense.

Suspense is the degree to which vacuums are stretched before any fulfilment occurs.

On his way out, we are given one further chilling prompt when the signalman asks a parting question:

> 'What made you cry, "Halloa! Below there!" to-night?'

> 'Heaven knows,' said I. 'I cried something to that effect—'

> 'Not to that effect, sir. Those were the very words. I know them well.'

'Admit those were the very words. I said them, no doubt, because I saw you below.'

'For no other reason?'

'What other reason could I possibly have?'

'You had no feeling that they were conveyed to you in any supernatural way?'

'No.'

This interchange of short questions and answers serves to undermine the certainties about the signalman that we may have developed up to this point. It's a technique Dickens uses throughout the story, as when the narrator returns and the signalman begins telling him of his 'trouble':

'That mistake?'

'No. That some one else.'

'Who is it?'

'I don't know.'

'Like me?'

'I don't know. I never saw the face. The left arm is across the face, and the right arm is waved,--violently waved. This way.'

I followed his action with my eyes, and it was the action of an arm gesticulating, with the utmost passion and vehemence, 'For God's sake, clear the way!'

The short, punchy sentences, the tense question-and-answer exchanges, punctuate the mystery vacuum. We listen, with the narrator, to the tale of spectral appearances. We resist, with the narrator, any supernatural conclusions: 'Resisting the slow touch of a frozen finger tracing out my spine, I showed him how that this figure must be a deception of his sense of sight'. But these 'rational' interruptions are a device that Dickens is using to amplify the tension.

We are glued by the powerful mystery vacuum to the signalman's tale now, our remaining resistance mirrored explicitly by the narrator:

> But he would beg to remark that he had not finished.

> I asked his pardon, and he slowly added these words, touching my arm, --

> 'Within six hours after the Appearance, the memorable accident on this Line happened, and within ten hours the dead and wounded were brought along through the tunnel over the spot where the figure had stood.'

> A disagreeable shudder crept over me, but I did my best against it.

Again, the narrator interrupts; again, the signalman says he has not finished: "'This,' he said, again laying his hand upon my arm, and glancing over his shoulder with hollow eyes, ' was just a year ago.' '

The contact between narrator and signalman is now physical. And again we have a series of nervous questions:

> 'Did it cry out?'

> 'No. It was silent.'

> 'Did it wave its arm?'

> 'No. It leaned against the shaft of the light, with both hands before the face. Like this.'

> Once more I followed his action with my eyes. It was an action of mourning. I have seen such an attitude in stone figures on tombs.

The reference to tombs is, of course, not accidental: it is an image which taps into basic vacuums of life and death. When the signalman tells of further apparitions and of the "'beautiful young lady'" who "' had died instantaneously in one of the compartments, and was brought in here, and laid down on this floor between us'" the reaction has become a physical action:

Involuntarily I pushed my chair back, as I looked from the boards at which he pointed to himself.

'True, sir. True. Precisely as it happened, so I tell it you.'

Now that the narrator's reasoning powers have failed him, Dickens turns up the volume literally by having the setting step in to create further mood music: 'I could think of nothing to say, to any purpose, and my mouth was very dry. The wind and the wires took up the story with a long lamenting wail.'

Note that the sound isn't a 'long, humming crescendo' or a 'long, buzzing background noise': Dickens is too much of a master author not to make use of further imagery associated with basic vacuums of life and loss: it's a 'lamenting wail' that the narrator hears. The narrator is now determined to act. He persuades the signalman to look with him for the ghost at the tunnel mouth, the physical embodiment of the vacuums of the story:

> I opened the door, and stood on the step, while he stood in the doorway. There was the Danger-light. There was the dismal mouth of the tunnel. There were the high, wet stone walls of the cutting. There were the stars above them.

Short, crisp, statements that serve to punctuate the scene - each one a short breath long.

When the narrator leaves again, unsure of what to do, his discomfiture has a point to focus on: 'That I more than once looked back at the red light as I ascended the pathway, that I did not like the red light, and that I should have slept but poorly if my bed had been under it, I see no reason to conceal.' But Dickens has now added a deeper, moral dimension, further drawing in the deeper level of basic vacuum power. The narrator - and to that degree we as readers - are concerned about responsibilities and outcomes:

> But what ran most in my thoughts was the consideration how ought I to act, having become the recipient of this disclosure? I had proved the man to be intelligent, vigilant, painstaking, and exact; but how long might he remain so, in his state of mind? Though in a subordinate position, still he held a most important trust, and would I (for instance) like to stake my own life on the chances of his continuing to execute it with precision?

Having laboured to create an effective mystery, Dickens now points us in the direction of an uncertainty: while we wonder about the nature, origin and meaning of the spectre, we are now anxious about the consequences. These are distinctly different vectors: the mystery vacuum 'glues' us to the story; the moral vacuum suggested by the question of responsibility drives us forward towards a resolution of some kind. Together they intensify the tension.

Tension measures the size of the vacuums created before fulfilment occurs.

When we see what the narrator sees on his return to the site the next day, we experience a chill:

> Before pursuing my stroll, I stepped to the brink, and mechanically looked down, from the point from which I had first seen him. I cannot describe the thrill that seized upon me, when, close at the mouth of the tunnel, I saw the appearance of a man, with his left sleeve across his eyes, passionately waving his right arm.

What follows is a resolution of events, fulfilling the linear vacuum of 'What happens next?' - the train has run over the signalman, killing him; the 'ghost' was a kind of premonition - but not a resolution of the mystery vacuum of 'What is going on?'. The narrator explicitly has no answers to those - true Ironies never do - and concludes by pointing out that the words he attached (but never voiced) to the gestures of the spectre - 'Below there! Look out! Look out! For God's sake, clear the way!' - turn out to be the words actually used by the train driver in his attempt to warn the signalman. This final, chilling reminder connects us through the narrator to the events of the tale and removes any kind of rational conjecture we might have had: how could the workings of the narrator's own mind have been so uncannily reflected in the events we have witnessed?

Our mystery vacuum is filled by an icy cold vision which effectively explains nothing. It is Dickens' final masterstroke in a triumph of short story telling, pushing the finger of the spectre not only before our faces as readers but into our very souls.

Successful authors of Comedies or Epics employ the vacuums of disharmony, disappointment, lack of fulfilment, to set the reader up for the 'joy' of a restored harmony and filled vacuum; authors of

Tragedies and Ironies use the same methods, but, while they naturally wrap up the linear vacuums of the plot, bringing their tales to some kind of conclusion, they leave the reader with unanswered questions and only partly fill, or hint at, the fulfilment of mystery vacuums.

Emotional ups and downs in stories are really the outward signs of vacuum manipulation on many levels.

A whole further book could be written just about Stage 5, the use of vacuums at word and sentence level. Stage 5's stylistic techniques convey the full power of the bridging vacuums of Stage 4, which create a channel to the structural plot and character vacuums of your basic work in Stage 3. Putting all this together, you are no longer merely 'writing ideas down on the page', you are engineering a piece of fiction using precise tools.

A story is an attention-capturing device which uses words and vacuums.

Note a key mechanical fact: most readers read at the pace of about one page every two minutes. Some are faster, of course, and some slower, but experience suggests that two minutes per page is about average. So, three minutes probably takes your reader somewhere onto page two. Those first two pages are where something vital needs to happen if you are going to continue to keep the reader's attention.

You need to have effective vacuums at work in the first two pages, ideally in your opening sentence.

Then you need to use the same principles throughout your work. All great authors do this, from Hemingway to Tolkien, from Shakespeare to the Beowulf poet: precise word choice, precise plot structuring, rhythmic back and forth, strength and weakness, horror and comedy, emphasis and non-emphasis, long sentences, short sentences, from the level of words all the way up to the work as a whole.

If you create the ongoing presence of vacuums in your work, starting at a word level, progressing up through a sentence level and then within paragraphs, you will keep a firm grip on your reader's 'hand' throughout the work. Contrast creates vacuums - stark contrast increases pace, subtle contrast decreases pace, ridiculous contrast creates humour, expected contrast creates seriousness.

Create vacuums on every level.

Vacuums in Chapter Two of 'The Lord of the Rings'

Here is another example of Stage 5 techniques at work in Chapter Two of *The Lord of the Rings,* called 'The Shadow of the Past'. In this part of the story, old man archetype the wizard Gandalf returns to visit young, orphaned protagonist Frodo. From the moment they greet each other there is a carefully controlled pattern of vacuums which rhythmically eases the reader along through the entire chapter.

> They looked hard at one another. 'Ah well eh?' said Gandalf. 'You look the same as ever, Frodo!'

> 'So do you,' Frodo replied; but secretly he thought that Gandalf looked older and more careworn.

Immediately, a counter-balance of vacuums is invoked: Gandalf looks 'the same as ever' in the form of Frodo's polite greeting, but 'secretly' looks 'older and more careworn'. Why? This is a subtle mystery vacuum as well as outlining a possible character vacuum for Gandalf - what is weighing the wizard down so much?

The gentle contrasts continue in nearly every sentence, almost subliminally, until the reader is lulled:

> A bright fire was on the hearth, but the sun was warm, and the wind was in the South. (*A linear vacuum contrasting the warmth outside with the need for a fire indoors.*)

> (Gandalf's) hair was perhaps whiter than it had been then, and his beard and eyebrows were perhaps longer, and his face more lined with care and wisdom (*character vacuum*); but his eyes were as bright as ever, and he smoked and blew smoke rings with the same vigour and delight (*a contrast serving to highlight the prior vacuum*).

> Even in the light of morning (Frodo) felt the dark shadow of the tidings that Gandalf had brought (*the contrast again serving to highlight the vacuum of the 'dark shadow'*).

Gandalf then begins to relate to Frodo the details of the Ring's history and its terrible nature. After Gandalf explains that the Ring will wear down any wearer until he is spiritually eroded, and 'sooner or later the dark power will devour him', Frodo's response is: "How terrifying!" After a long silence, this is contrasted with one of the most unexpected and innocent sounds in the world: 'The sound of Sam Gamgee cutting the lawn came in from the garden.'

Each subtle positive moment - the conversational banter, the sun outside, the sound of cutting the lawn - serves a purpose: to highlight the vacuums with which they contrast.

At no point does Tolkien let our attention waver from the tense mood of the darkened room inside Frodo's home where this conversation is taking place - but he actually increases the tension and makes it more effective by rhythmically contrasting it with other, lighter and more innocent details around it. This contrast is made implicit in the symbol of the Ring itself - '"Bilbo thought the ring was very beautiful, and very useful at need"' explains the wizard - and in the sharp distinction between the largely comic world of the hobbits and the darker forces at work elsewhere in Tolkien's world:

> 'Ever since Bilbo left I have been deeply concerned about you, and about all these charming, absurd, helpless hobbits. It would be a grievous blow to the world, if the Dark Power overcame the Shire; if all your kind, jolly, stupid Bolgers, Hornblowers, Boffins, Bracegirdles, and the rest, not to mention the ridiculous Bagginses, became enslaved.'

Even as Gandalf tells Frodo all this, and then submits the Ring to an alarming test by throwing it into the fire, the author points gently to contrasting factors: 'The room became dark and silent, though the clack of Sam's shears, now nearer to the windows, could still be heard faintly from the garden.'

Contrasts continue as Gandalf outlines the character of Gollum for Frodo, and attempts to explain his lust for the Ring:

> 'He hated the dark, and he hated light more: he hated everything, and the Ring most of all.'

'What do you mean?' said Frodo. 'Surely the Ring was his precious and the only thing he cared for? But if he hated it, why didn't he get rid of it, or go away and leave it?'

'You ought to begin to understand, Frodo, after all you have heard,' said Gandalf. 'He hated it and loved it, as he hated and loved himself. He could not get rid of it. He had no will left in the matter.'

Having heard the full history of the Ring from the wizard, Frodo, afraid of his burden, offers it to him, and Gandalf's fearful refusal is swiftly juxtaposed with something quite different:

'Do not tempt me! For I do not wish to become like the Dark Lord himself. Yet the way of the Ring to my heart is by pity, pity for weakness and the desire of strength to do good. Do not tempt me! I dare not take it, not even to keep it safe, unused. The wish to wield it would be too great, for my strength. I shall have such need of it. Great perils lie before me.' He went to the window and drew aside the curtains and the shutters. Sunlight streamed back again into the room. Sam passed along the path outside whistling.

As Frodo reaches a decision about what to do, explicit use is made of the difference between the inside of the room in which the discussion has taken place and the much brighter outside: '"No!" answered Frodo, coming back to himself out of darkness, and finding to his surprise that it was not dark, and that out of the window he could see the sunlit garden.'

The Ring, of course, is a perfect symbolic vacuum: an empty circle, which threatens to suck into it the whole world. It operates on character, affecting each person who comes near it; it is central to the plot, creating the entire linear vacuum of the story; it resonates with mystery, in that we are never certain of its power or how active it is. In one simple object, Tolkien captured all the vacuum power that he needed to drive his story forward and keep our attention glued to it.

The chapter concludes with Sam Gamgee, Frodo's servant (a classic comic companion who later saves the day, playing a pivotal role in the quest and the story as a whole) being drawn into the room by Gandalf, who commands him to go with Frodo - but even this final sentence is told in contrasts: "'Me go and see Elves and all! Hooray!" he shouted, and then burst into tears.'

Vacuums, used in this way on a word and sentence level, have ensured, amongst other things, that the wild and hard-to-believe back-story of the Ring and the whole host of larger than life characters and events which it introduces draw our attention in such a way that we don't reject them out of hand - a master author like Tolkien knows how to use them to bring about a smooth gradient so that, almost before we know it, we have been 'captured'.

Vacuums in Chapter One of 'Voyage to Venus'

The work of Tolkien's compatriot, C. S. Lewis, can similarly serve as a good example of Stage 5 techniques in operation.

Voyage to Venus, or *Perelandra* as it was originally called, provides in its opening chapter a perfect example of an author progressing from an accepted and ordinary reality that might be shared with readers - starting with vague feelings of discomfort or inconvenience that readers would recognise - to an encounter with the supernatural which would undoubtedly be outside most people's experience. In this way, the reader is drawn into the novel and moved from the Ironic stagework of the modern reader, in which experience is interpreted subjectively and psychologically, into the genre of Epic, in which real, objective forces are at work. Lewis does this with such skill that, like most fiction from great writers, we barely notice the progression.

Chapter One begins with the author inserting himself as the first person narrator of a story in which he makes no appearance beyond the first chapter. Purposefully, we begin with the narrator's very ordinary walk from a railway station to visit his friend Dr. Elwin Ransom. Informed readers will know that Ransom has visited the planet Mars (or Malacandra) in the earlier book in the trilogy, *Out of the Silent Planet,* but new readers require no knowledge of that back-story to be affected by Lewis's techniques:

> As I left the railway station at Worchester and set out on the three-mile walk to Ransom's cottage, I reflected that no one on that platform could possibly guess the truth about the man I was going to visit. The flat heath which spread out before me (for the village lies all behind and to the north of the station)

looked an ordinary heath. The gloomy five-o'clock sky was such as you might see on any autumn afternoon. The few houses and the clumps of red or yellowish trees were in no way remarkable.

Our attention is directed to very normal, earthly things before Lewis gives us a quick summary of Ransom's earlier adventure:

Who could imagine that a little farther on in that quiet landscape I should meet and shake by the hand a man who had lived and eaten and drunk in a world forty million miles distant from London, who had seen this Earth from where it looks like a mere point of green fire, and who had spoken face to face with a creature whose life began before our own planet was inhabitable?

What Lewis then does is present that contrast - the void between the ordinary things we know and the utterly incredible things that we have no experience of, including meetings with the cosmic beings called 'eldils', the equivalent of angels in the story - in degrees of increasing psychological realism as Lewis-as-narrator heads down the road towards Ransom's cottage:

At present I was going to see Ransom in answer to a wire which had said 'Come down Thursday if possible. Business.' I guessed what sort of business he meant, and that was why I kept on telling myself that it would be perfectly delightful to spend a night with Ransom and also kept on feeling that I was not enjoying the prospect as much as I ought to. It was the eldila that were my trouble. I could just get used to the fact that Ransom had been to Mars ... but to have met an eldil, to have spoken with something whose life appeared to be practically unending.

The chapter is composed of a rhythmic switching between the ordinary and the extra-ordinary in the narrator's mind (and therefore for the reader). In terms of vacuums, we start with additional, minor vacuums, but these are contrasted with larger, essential vacuums to do with life, death and the fate of worlds. Lewis is very aware that initially at least he must phrase the Lewis-as-narrator voice using psychological terms:

As I plodded along the empty, unfenced road which runs across the middle of Worchester Common I tried to dispel my growing sense of malaise by analysing it. What, after all, was I afraid of? The moment I had put this question I regretted it. I was shocked to find that I had mentally used the word 'afraid'. Up till then I had tried to pretend that I was feeling only distaste, or embarrassment, or even boredom. But the mere word afraid had let the cat out of the bag. I realised now that my emotion was neither more, nor less, nor other, than fear.

Lewis-as-narrator then outlines his fear and in doing so explicitly brings together the 'normal' world of the reader with its recognisable minor inconveniences or unwanted sensations and the 'supernatural' world into which he is attempting to draw him or her:

The truth was that all I heard about them served to connect two things which one's mind tends to keep separate, and that connecting gave one a sort of shock. We tend to think about non-human intelligences in two distinct categories which we label 'normal' and 'supernatural' respectively. We think, in one mood, of Mr. Wells' Martians (very unlike the real Malacandrians, by ' the bye), or his Selenites. In quite a different mood we let our minds loose on the possibility of angels, ghosts, fairies, and the like. But the very moment we are compelled to recognise a creature in either class as real the distinction begins to get blurred: and when it is a creature like an eldil the distinction vanishes altogether. These things were not animals-to that extent one had to classify them with the second group; but they had some kind of material vehicle whose presence could (in principle) be scientifically verified. To that extent they belonged to the first group. The distinction between natural and supernatural, in fact, broke down; and when it had done so, one realised how great a comfort it had been-how it had eased the burden of intolerable strangeness which this universe imposes on us by dividing it into two halves and encouraging the mind never to think of both in the same context.

This important philosophic connection is actually a connection between universal or lighter vacuums and basic or much heavier and more significant vacuums, too large and perhaps ponderous for an ordinary reader. Lewis-as-writer immediately undercuts the image with a reference to something very down-to-earth:

'This is a long, dreary road,' I thought to myself. 'Thank goodness I haven't anything to carry.' And then, with a start of realisation, I remembered that I ought to be carrying a pack, containing my things for the night. I swore to myself. I must have left the thing in the train. Will you believe me when I say that my immediate impulse was to turn back to the station and 'do something about it'? Of course there was nothing to be done which could not equally well be done by ringing up from the cottage. That train, with my pack in it, must by this time be miles away.

Lewis-as-narrator persuades himself to go on, but it 'was such hard work that I felt as if I were walking against a headwind; but in fact it was one of those still, dead evenings when no twig stirs, and beginning to be a little foggy.' This is word- and sentence-level mastery: not only is our attention as readers drawn out of the internal debate in the narrator's mind and placed on the apparently very real and commonplace environment through which the narrator is moving, but the choice of words - 'still', 'dead', 'stirs', 'foggy' - continues to resonate with the fear that Lewis-as-writer has managed to conjure. In other words, having connected up the larger vacuums, Lewis makes sure that he keeps that connection 'live' with appropriate use of words.

What happens to the modern mind when confronted by vacuums of this immensity? Lewis-as-narrator becomes so anxious in pondering the eldils and all that they link with in his mind, that he verges on the edge of a breakdown, or at least on the point of fleeing the scene:

How if my friend were the unwitting bridge, the Trojan Horse, whereby some possible invader were effecting its landing on Tellus? And then once more, just as when I had discovered that I had to pack, the impulse to go no farther returned to me. "Go back, go back," it whispered to me, "send him a wire, tell him you were ill, say you'll come some other time - anything."

Lewis-as-narrator reasons himself into returning home and avoiding the visit altogether:

My only sensible course was to turn back at once and get safe home, before I lost my memory or became hysterical, and to put myself in the hands of a doctor. It was sheer madness to go on.

Lewis-as-writer ensures that he still has a grip on us as readers by again referring to the external scenery at this point:

> I was now coming to the end of the heath and going down a small hill, with a copse on my left and some apparently deserted industrial buildings on my right. At the bottom the evening mist was partly thick.

This rhythmic referral to the commonplace and external is never coincidental in the hands of a great writer. It serves both to anchor the reader's attention and to highlight the contrast with the uncommon. Quickening the pace, Lewis-as-writer switches straight away back to the conflict in Lewis-as-narrator's mind:

> They call it a Breakdown at first. Wasn't there some mental disease in which quite ordinary objects looked to the patient unbelievably ominous?...looked, in fact, just as that abandoned factory looks to me now? Great bulbous shapes of cement, strange brickwork bogeys, glowered at me over dry scrubby grass pock-marked with grey pools and intersected with the remains of a light railway.

Lewis-as-narrator persuades himself to continue towards Ransom's cottage, but the switching back and forth between external, ordinary objects and internal, psychological horror is swifter now:

> I was past the dead factory now, down in the fog, where it was very cold. Then came a moment - the first one - of absolute terror and I had to bite my lip to keep myself from screaming. It was only a cat that had run across the road, but I found myself completely unnerved. "Soon you will really be screaming," said my inner tormentor, "running round and round, screaming, and you won't be able to stop it."

This increases until, in Lewis-as-narrator's mind and in ours as readers, the outer and the inner world are explicitly conflated:

> We have all known times when inanimate objects seemed to have almost a facial expression, and it was the expression of this bit of road which I did not like. "It's not true," said my mind, "that people who are really going mad never think they're going mad." Suppose that real insanity had chosen this place in which to begin? In that case, of course, the black enmity of those

dripping trees-their horrible expectancy-would be a hallucination.

Such is the terror painted for us in words that Lewis-as-writer and Lewis-as-narrator merge in order to get the reader through to the door of the cottage. This isn't an accident: Lewis is using a technique here, combining forces to create a more powerful drive which will literally pull the reader through:

> I have naturally no wish to enlarge on this phase of my story. The state of mind I was in was one which I look back on with humiliation. I would have passed it over if I did not think that some account of it was necessary for a full understanding of what follows-and, perhaps, of some other things as well. At all events, I can't really describe how I reached the front door of the cottage. Somehow or other, despite the loathing and dismay that pulled me back and a sort of invisible wall of resistance that met me in the face, fighting for each step, and almost shrieking as a harmless spray of the hedge touched my face, I managed to get through the gate and up the little path. And there I was, drumming on the door and wringing the handle and shouting to him to let me in as if my life depended on it.

All this has served to link in us, the readers, a vacuum of great size: an emptiness, a mystery, an unknown, which craves to be filled, to be solved. As Lewis the narrator fumbles with a match to see what he has stumbled on in Ransom's cottage, so we as readers are desperate for light to be cast on the scene. In a masterstroke, the one flash of light from the narrator's flickering match reveals a coffin-shaped object on the floor. Coffins equal death equal horror, tapping into dark basic vacuums that we try to avoid thinking about normally.

This isn't a horror story, however. Lewis isn't writing an Irony: quite the opposite. He doesn't want this hole in our knowledge to be filled only with dark thoughts - just, for the moment, an unutterable strangeness. Instead of dwelling too much on the image of the coffin, our attention is immediately directed to the thing which Lewis-as-narrator has been keen to avoid, but we as readers (from the safety of our own armchairs) have been keen to meet: an eldil.

> It was perfectly articulate: it was even, I suppose, rather beautiful. But it was, if you understand me, inorganic. We feel the difference between animal voices (including those of the

human animal) and all other noises pretty clearly, I fancy, though it is hard to define. Blood and lungs and the warm, moist cavity of the mouth are somehow indicated in every Voice. Here they were not. The two syllables sounded more as if they were played on an instrument than as if they were spoken: and yet they did not sound mechanical either. A machine is something we make out of natural materials, this was more as if rock or crystal or light had spoken of itself. And it went through me from chest to groin like the thrill that goes through you when you think you have lost your hold while climbing a cliff.

Lewis-as-narrator struggles to put the experience into words, but gives us just enough for some kind of vicarious experience to be shared. Deftly, Lewis-as-writer then shifts our attention onto another kind of vacuum, a moral vacuum:

I felt sure that the creature was what we call 'good', but I wasn't sure whether I liked 'goodness' so much as I had supposed. This is a very terrible experience. As long as what you are afraid of is something evil, you may still hope that the good may come to your rescue. But suppose you struggle through to the good and find that it also is dreadful?

Our attention as readers has been gripped so thoroughly throughout this chapter that we, just like Lewis-as-narrator, have been 'drawn in' to the story:

Oddly enough my very sense of helplessness saved me and steadied me. For now I was quite obviously 'drawn in'. The struggle was over. The next decision did not lie with me.

Now we are ready to meet the story's real protagonist, and this is the exact point at which Ransom makes his entrance. In this way, Lewis shifts us from the empty horror of an Irony, with no solutions and the ordered world subverted ('suppose you struggle through to the good and find that it also is dreadful?') into the providential world of an Epic. We discover early in the next chapter that what seemed purely psychological terrors in Lewis-as-narrator's mind were actually externally-sourced thoughts, planted there by dark forces.

'By Jove, I'm glad to see you,' said Ransom, advancing and shaking hands with me. 'I'd hoped to be able to meet you at the station, but everything has had to be arranged in such a hurry and I found at the last moment that I'd got to go up to Cambridge. I never intended to leave you to make that journey alone.' Then, seeing, I suppose, that I was still staring at him rather stupidly, he added, 'I say-you're all right, aren't you? You got through the barrage without any damage?'

'The barrage?-I don't understand.'

'I was thinking you would have met some difficulties in getting here.'

'Oh, that,' said I. 'You mean it wasn't just my nerves? There really was something in the way?'

'Yes. They didn't want you to get here. I was afraid something of the sort might happen but there was no time to do anything about it. I was pretty sure you'd get through somehow.'

We have moved out of the realms of Irony and into a wholly different genre, guided all the way by a master author.

Stage 5 Fulfilment

Examples of Stage 5 power are as numerous as there are works of fiction. Any work that truly masters Stage 5 usage will guarantee its future for some time to come. Why? Because Stage 5 vacuum power, properly used, enables the work to reach into the worlds of people who haven't committed anything consciously at all to the work, without any effort at all, and with very little time investment. This means that your work can contact and engage with a reader who has *little or no awareness of need*, without risking anything. Remember those people? They are the ones whose attention is still in a plasma state, floating around, not particularly flowing towards anything. Stage 5 vacuum power can attract their attention because there are no apparent barriers at all.

Obviously and importantly, Stage 5 work must contain *real value*. It would do no good at all - and would probably be detrimental - if the sentence-level work was poorly presented or contained boring, run-of-the-mill clichés; it would be useless if the wordage was weak of even inaccurate; it would be pointless if the dialogue wasn't put together properly and sensitively. Stage 5 work is a real chance to give people something of real worth. And of course Stage 5 is where the actual writing takes place - putting words and sentences together to create mini-vacuums is what successful writers do. Without a working Stage 5, all you have is a flat set of notes.

Stage 5 is your communication line to actual readers.

Stages 3, 4 and 5 could form the basis for a whole new type of fiction for you, a completely new way of working. Using them, you would be employing vacuum power to bring about affluence for you as a writer and for your readers in terms of effects created.

Chapter Sixteen:
Fitting the Stages Together

So you can see now how these five stages work together. Looking at the sequence in reverse, using another analogy, will hopefully make this even clearer:

Stage 5 contains the page-level *seeds* which you have planted which can stir vacuums into life (or condense readers' 'attention plasma' into 'liquid').

Stage 4 contains the growing seedlings which fill real vacuums for real readers. Vacuums have now worked to 'liquify' attention and make it flow.

Stage 3 is the strong growing plant, the full work which is your staple, creating and filling character, linear, moral and core vacuums on a regular basis.

Stage 2 is the branching tree that takes what you do to a higher level and generates a whole new range of reader satisfaction and meaning by producing the 'fruit' of fulfilled core vacuums.

Stage 1, the writer, breathes continuing life into the other stages and, by aligning all of the above, ensures a powerful lingering effect upon the reader. To extend the gardening analogy, the writer tends the garden in which he or she has grown the tree. But the forest surrounding one work contains the mysterious network of interconnections which will forever sustain the reader or any critic.

This is the vacuum-based new Five Stage Fiction Model which, if applied correctly, will transform your writing entirely.

You can tackle creating a work from both ends of these stages: some writers begin with the word-sentence-page interface of Stage 5 and work up to and around the rest of the Stages as they go - though it's probably true to say that 90% of would-be writers fail to recognise that these stages even exist, and fall into the galaxy-sized hole of 'one idea after another' in the hope of capturing reader attention. The product of this approach is often directionless wordage which requires a real effort to read - and that's because the reader has to supply the effort: the story lacks vacuum power of its own.

Other writers start from the other end, developing powerful and deeply significant core vacuums and then breaking them down into some kind of story structure through Stages 2 and 3 - but many of these often fail because they do not see the skills needed to accomplish Stages 4 and 5. The product of this approach is profound writing which misses its audience and reads drily, like an essay or other non-fiction work.

Working on all five Stages creates successful works of fiction which convey powerful ideas and feelings to a growing audience of readers and re-readers.

Conventional fiction writing advice is largely based on the reader as a *passive, inert object*. The purpose of all creative writing in the traditional model is 'to spark the reader to life', hold that life and channel it, and then magnify that tentative, precarious 'flame' into a commitment.

It sounds workable - but it is so energy-intensive, so demanding and ultimately so fundamentally flawed that it exhausts most writers before they can convert enough 'inert matter' into life. It's an unhelpful model that fails to describe exactly what is happening.

It's the writer-centric, 'Life started with a spark' model which places your work at the core of the universe and seeks readers in the 'outer space' of the world at large.

In conventional models, reader commitment (it's said) is brought about by a quantity of stylistic features ('Let's push the fantastic features of our writing! If we do that in enough volume, people will be compelled to emotionally commit!'), by branding ('If we get our name known to enough people in enough places and contexts, people will be bound to commit!'), and so forth. These ideas are based on the overall notion that 'More equals good' and the hope that the more data or technique that is pumped into the piece of work, the more readers will commit. It's a Stage 5-based model.

Of course style, branding and so forth all has its place in Stage 5. But what makes successful fiction work is that there are other stages functioning behind the scenes.

Writing based on 'hot buttons', particular kinds of added value, using logic, emotion or personality, or making sure that your work has a particular structure, or providing data and correct links and so forth - all of these things are designed to give the 'passive reader' the information necessary to evaluate whether he or she wants to make an emotional commitment. What you may not initially see are the basic things which make this approach fundamentally flawed and which mean that, using this model, writers run out of money and energy before they complete any work of fiction.

Proper vacuum-powered fiction is based on a *completely different notion of what a reader is.* Instead of seeing readers as passive, inert objects who have to be pushed and shoved and attracted and moved and channeled, almost against their will, genuine vacuum-powered fiction sees them as *bursting with life and energy in the form of active, vibrant and powerful vacuums.*

If a writer can create a work which mirrors these vibrant, powerful vacuums, the reader won't have to expend any effort to read the story. Quite the opposite.

Character, linear, mystery, moral and core vacuums are the source of all the energy and work your work will ever need.

Here are the steps to take, simply put:

Step 1: Have enough confidence in yourself as a writer.

You have the power to create, select and develop vacuums. This is what it takes to write successful fiction.

Your ideas are the flesh that hides the bones of these vacuums.

That's Stage 1.

Step 2: Ensure that you have a core vacuum (or set of core vacuums) and something to fill it that fully satisfies a need (or, if you want to write a Tragedy or Irony, define it clearly and leave it empty).

There's nothing more important than developing a meaningful core vacuum. Fundamentally, this is the thing which will guarantee your ongoing success.

Any work of fiction is capable of generating emotion if the core vacuum is strong enough and the fulfilment accurate enough.

Step 3: Develop a character vacuum in proximity to your potential readers that mirrors the readers' exact needs.

This is the beginning of crafting a protagonist whose character acts as a magnet for the reader simply because he or she is *missing so much*. Start with a lighter, universal vacuum, and only hint at the deeper needs beneath it. Then build linear, mystery and moral vacuums around this central character.

Add in the archetypal companion characters as needed. You're putting together a machine which will grip and hold reader attention throughout the tale.

That's Stage 3.

Vacuums set up in a correct design will channel some of rushing river of readers through your work to fulfilment. Present a series of ever larger vacuums, leading straight to your core.

Step 4: Decide where you want your readers to come from.

As we have seen, there is really no shortage of readers. Almost everyone is a potential reader for something. Your problem is not a reader shortage but a problem with *work design*, or with *vacuums*.

All you need is *vacuums* to tap into any defined audience. Work over the universal vacuums you have come up with in Stage 3 and tailor them as much as you can to fit the kind of reader you want to appeal to.

That's Stage 4.

Step 5: Immediately fulfill a minor exact need.

Stage 5 exists to *capture attention page by page*. It is the thing which takes some of the reader's faint and perhaps wandering 'plasma' of attention and turns it into 'liquid' right from your opening sentence. It has to hit hard and accurately and it has to satisfy - it can't afford to miss the mark.

The very first page of your work, its opening sentence, has to be vacuum-charged.

The more vacuums you fill through this initial contact, the more successful you will be.

Until you hook a reader into the story, you still have no readers. You have a lot of *potential* readers whose vacuums have stuck to your work in the form of some attention. Someone has touched your work, lifted the book from a shelf. You have contacted a real potential reader. Use word and sentence level vacuum techniques to cool that attention plasma. Connect the reader up with the character vacuums of a protagonist in the first couple of pages, and you're off.

Stage 5 ignites the machine.

Conclusion

If you're a writer, or you want to be one, the product of this book should be that you want to write more. Hopefully, you have learned enough about how stories really work to now write something that someone else will want to read, will find fulfilling, and will pay you money for.

If you aren't actually writing, you can perhaps now see why. If your life is swallowed up by work, by children, by routines and relationships and so on, then these factors have to be outweighed by your own desire to write - your own character vacuum, if you like.

If your existing fiction sounded trite, boring, full of clichés, wandering everywhere, lacking drama and a proper ending, you now know why. You now have the tools to make characters leap into life; you have the techniques to invent dialogue and plots that are energised and magnetic.

If you are writing, and have produced something reasonable, you can perhaps now understand the rejection letters - and do something about them.

You now know that the statement in the first chapter of this book is true:

You can be a writer, and you can be successful; you can spot exactly what's wrong with your writing and fix it: your work can be moulded into shape and it can be made attractive to others, even publishers.

Your *desire* for a piece of fiction will be the thing that ensures that your ideas actually begin to turn into reality. You have to be committed, but at least you now have a grasp of the sequence that makes the working machine called a successful story.

You also now have criteria to judge the quality of what you're doing, perhaps for the first time. And that means that you're more likely to get the sense of *fulfilment* that you have always wanted to have as the writer of stories that work, and to be able to produce that sense of fulfilment in others.

You should also now be aware of what it is going to take to move your work to the right along the Spectrum of Fiction above, so that you are actually writing effectively for readers.

Now there's only really one question left for you to answer:

'What effect do you want to create for the reader?'

This isn't really a conclusion, but a potential new beginning.

What should you do next?

Here are some suggestions:

The following Self Assessment Questionnaire will give you a much better idea now of where your operation lacks vacuum power - as well as where vacuum power is strongest in your work.

Then it's up to you to do the work needed to transform your work into the Five Stage Model, a reader-centric machine which will save you time and effort and possibly multiply your income many times over.

If you need any help in doing this, the companion volume to this book, *How Stories Really Work - A Practical Manual to Transform Your Fiction* - takes the material of these chapters and transforms it into step-by-step exercises which gradually build the Five Stage Model around your work. If you need more help, the *How to Write Stories That Work - and Get Them Published!* e-course will walk you through every step, accompanied by diagrams and exercises and personal, tailor-made feedback until you have a published work in your hands.

By visiting the Clarendon House Publications website you can also get additional assistance, including general advice which will point your work in the right direction for success, and even a tailor-made, comprehensive programme of help for your fiction including an Ideas Workshop, guidance with character construction, support with attracting readers, advice on how to obtain emotional commitment, and help with plot structuring, quality of style and fulfilling reader expectations.

Clarendon House Publications also offers full proofreading and editing services, and preparations for publication including formatting, page numbering and so on.

Clarendon House Publications can even help to get you published to your exact specifications and offers a marketing programme (with options to appear on Amazon, Barnes & Noble, etc) as well as bonus material on how to succeed in business as a writer and how to achieve your personal goals.

Simply visit

www.clarendonhousebooks.com

or email me at

grant@clarendonhousebooks.com

for details.

You can also give any feedback, including success stories, via the website.

Based on what you have to say, future editions of these materials can be tweaked to better suit your needs and the needs of others.

I look forward to hearing from you!

-Grant P. Hudson

Acknowledgements

As I've said before, fiction is a field with many authorities in it much more learned and wise and well-read than myself, the prime one being the Canadian academic Northrop Frye, whose book *Anatomy of Criticism* first showed me that I was not alone in my speculations about literature. J. R. R. Tolkien helped in the early days through his work, and enormous incentive was gained from the writings of C. S. Lewis. More recently, Christopher Booker's *Seven Basic Plots* re-opened my eyes, which were originally permitted to open when I began a thesis on Tolkien, Lewis and Ursula Le Guin many years ago in the English Department at Flinders University in South Australia, under the careful tutelage of Dr. Graham Tulloch. To all of these and many more I owe a great debt.

For patience in listening, I must thank my long-time friend and fellow student of these matters, Dr. J. Entwisle, and for the 'field trials' of a great deal of the ideas herein I owe much to many ever-attentive students who had to suffer through many lessons in which the principles of this work were honed and finalised.

Originally, of course, my interest in literature and the encouragement to read whatever I pleased came from my beloved father and mother.

The encouragement to eventually overcome years of procrastination, though, and to get this book done, I owe to my wife.

Fiction Self-Assessment Questionnaire

Fiction Self-Assessment Questionnaire

Introduction

This questionnaire is designed to give you an 'diagnostic analysis' of your fiction so that you can see its strengths and weaknesses and work out the key areas on which to focus. It consists of an 'X-Ray Analysis' which outlines every part of your work, helping you to spot the things you need to do to make your fiction more successful.

1. The X-Ray Analysis

To understand how this works and to explain why each one of these aspects of your fiction is important, let's refresh our memory as to how a cup of tea is made.

Making a Cup of Tea

Making a cup of tea begins with the idea of making a cup of tea.

Then there needs to be someone to make it.

There needs to be a desire for a cup of tea to ensure that the idea actually begins to turn into reality.

Certain materials are needed for the tea to be made: a kettle, a cup, the tea itself, milk and so forth. These have to be purchased.

Then the tea has to actually be made - in whatever sequence is preferred, milk in first or not.

The first sip tests the quality of the cup of tea.

Then the cup of tea is finally consumed.

It should be clear that if any one of these steps is not there, the whole product is not fully achieved.

Obviously, without the idea of making a cup of tea nothing even starts to happen.

If there's no one to make it, the idea won't get very far.

In the absence of any desire for a cup of tea, even if someone has the idea and there is someone to make it, there won't be sufficient motivation for anything to occur.

Without a kettle, a cup, the tea itself, milk and so on, there would be no cup of tea. If these can't be afforded, the idea stalls right there.

If the idea gets as far as this and the sequence of making it goes wrong, there goes the cup of tea.

If the quality of the cup of tea isn't good enough, it might as well not have been made.

And then, after all that, if the cup of tea sits untouched and unconsumed, the whole thing will have been a waste of time.

Each step, then, is essential.

What has this to do with your writing?

The idea of making a cup of tea is like the idea that underpins any piece of fiction. This is that part of the process which originates the whole thing and plans and directs the writing.

There needs to be someone to make the tea, and any piece of fiction requires people of one sort or another. This is the construction of characters or viewpoints.

The desire for a cup of tea reflects the desire that there must be in a reader if the fiction is to succeed. This involves developing attractive power.

Just as certain materials are needed for the tea to be made, any successful work of fiction needs emotional commitment on the part of readers. To acquire this, something needs to be paid out.

The tea has to actually be made and in any story something which we usually call a 'plot' has to be created, assembled, and moved forward in a particular sequence.

As the quality of the cup of tea must be assessed, so must any work of fiction have some way of judging the quality of what it is producing and delivering and ensuring that it matches the readers' needs. This is the fine tuning or quality of writing department, which includes the nebulous thing called 'style' and word- and sentence-level vacuums.

Consumption of the tea marks the end of the cycle, and in any story it is when the reader has finished reading, hopefully marking the closure of the matter. This is fulfilment.

Answer each of the following questions as honestly and thoroughly as you can and at the end you will be able to see exactly which areas of your writing are doing well and which are letting you down. You will notice that some of the questions address similar issues from slightly different angles. This is so that the analysis can get an overview of your concerns and a more accurate picture of where your fiction's strengths and weaknesses lie.

Of course, this is all based on your viewpoint and your answers, but because of the multiple questioning, it will produce a vital snapshot of where things are at right now.

Delete the answers which don't apply, leaving the one which you feel is most appropriate in response to the question.

MOSTLY YES = Y

SOMETIMES, MAYBE OR PARTLY = M

MOSTLY NO = N

1. As a writer, do you have well-laid-out plans for the next 5 to 10 years?

Y M N

2. Are you finding it difficult to develop convincing or attractive characters?

Y M N

3. Is your writing effectively bringing in droves of readers?

Y M N

4. Do you experience problems getting emotional commitment from readers?

Y M N

5. Are you happy with the plot structure of your work?

Y M N

6. Is your writing style of sufficient quality?

Y M N

7. Do your readers quickly appreciate what your work 'is all about'?

Y M N

8. Do you find it easy to set writing goals and work towards them?

Y M N

9. Do characters often seem weak or ineffective?

Y M N

10. Are you attracting lots of readers?

Y M N

11. Do you struggle to inject emotion into the story?

Y M N

12. Do you experience plot construction problems?

Y M N

13. Do you monitor the quality of your writing in some way?

Y M N

14. Are you able to deliver a powerful ending?

Y M N

15. Does your writing regularly meet targets?

Y M N

16. Do you have solid, realistic characters?

Y M N

17. Do you feel that trying to attract readers is a waste of time?

Y M N

18. Are you struggling emotionally with your work?

Y M N

19. Are you concerned about the motion of the plot?

Y M N

20. Do you have a definite style - a way of effectively communicating with readers?

Y M N

21. Do you suffer from problems to do with the ending of the story?

Y M N

22. Do you think your fiction reflects your vision of life?

Y M N

23. Are your characters generally working out?

Y M N

24. Have you got an active way of attracting readers and holding their attention effectively?

Y M N

25. Does your fiction have healthy emotional content which works on readers?

Y M N

26. Do you often make significant changes to the plot?

Y M N

27. Do you get many rejections?

Y M N

28. Do you set up the story well and then have trouble delivering?

Y M N

29. Are you in apathy about your writing?

Y M N

30. Are you confident that your characters have appeal?

Y M N

31. Are you troubled by a loss of readers?

Y M N

32. Do you feel your emotional content is about right?

Y M N

33. Is the plot exciting and effective in holding the reader's attention?

Y M N

34. Are there often questions from readers about what a particular sentence or section means?

Y M N

35. Is it hard to see how to wrap the story up?

Y M N

36. Are you happy with your writing?

Y M N

37. Do you have a method of keeping track of your characters' motivations?

Y M N

38. Do you feel that your story could be more targeted to a particular audience?

Y M N

39. Are you anxious about emotion in the story?

Y M N

40. Could the plot be speeded up?

Y M N

41. Have you developed a unique writing style?

Y M N

42. Do you have a number of ways of concluding the story?

Y M N

43. Are you overloaded or stressed by your writing?

Y M N

44. Do you understand your main characters' motivations entirely?

Y M N

45. Do you understand your readers?

Y M N

46. Does your story contain hardly any emotion?

Y M N

47. Have you ever 'walked through' the plot to make sure it makes sense?

Y M N

48. Is there a way of improving your writing style?

Y M N

49. Does your story conclude in such a way that readers have to work out their own ending?

Y M N

50. Do you have well-developed minor characters?

Y M N

51. Are your characters hard to motivate?

Y M N

52. Are you spending enough time on looking at things from the reader's point of view?

Y M N

53. Is it hard to make emotion work in your story?

Y M N

54. Are you confident enough in your style?

Y M N

55. Do you regularly review your ending to see if changes need to be made?

Y M N

56. Is your writing well known?

Y M N

57. Is there at least one character you are completely happy with?

Y M N

58. Do you write fiction easily?

Y M N

59. Do you have an effective set of characters?

Y M N

60. Is the emotional level lower than it should be?

Y M N

61. Is your plot disorganised?

Y M N

62. Is there room for improvement?

Y M N

63. Is your ending easily understandable even if it was translated into another language?

Y M N

64. Can you see yourself writing fiction for much longer?

Y M N

65. Do your characters work well together?

Y M N

66. Are you always worried about attracting readers?

Y M N

67. Is there an excess of emotion in the work?

Y M N

68. Do you have enough characters to produce a good story?

Y M N

69. Have you reached the top of your game?

Y M N

70. Is your writing universal (appealing to almost anyone)?

Y M N

Look over your answers and make sure that you have answered them as honestly and as accurately as possible, then proceed to scoring your answers.

SCORING SYSTEM

Here is the score sheet for your answers.

A. Carefully total up your overall score. You may be tempted to adjust some of your answers based on what you will now see as the 'correct' answer. Please don't! Only an honest assessment will be of any use to you.

	Y	M	N
1	10	5	0
2	0	5	10
3	10	5	0
4	0	5	10
5	10	5	0
6	10	5	0
7	10	5	0
8	10	5	0
9	0	5	10
10	10	5	0
11	0	5	10
12	0	5	10
13	10	5	0
14	10	5	0
15	10	5	0
16	10	5	0
17	0	5	10
18	0	5	10
19	0	5	10
20	10	5	0
21	0	5	10
22	10	5	0
23	10	5	0
24	10	5	0
25	10	5	0
26	0	5	10
27	0	5	10
28	0	5	10
29	0	5	10
30	10	5	0
31	0	5	10

32	10	5	0
33	10	5	0
34	0	5	10
35	0	5	10
36	10	5	0
37	10	5	0
38	0	5	10
39	0	5	10
40	0	5	10
41	10	5	0
42	10	5	0
43	0	5	10
44	10	5	0
45	10	5	0
46	0	5	10
47	10	5	0
48	10	5	0
49	10	5	0
50	10	5	0
51	0	5	10
52	10	5	0
53	0	5	10
54	10	5	0
55	10	5	0
56	10	5	0
57	10	5	0
58	10	5	0
59	10	5	0
60	0	5	10
61	0	5	10
62	0	5	10
63	10	5	0
64	10	5	0
65	10	5	0
66	0	5	10
67	10	5	0
68	10	5	0
69	0	5	10
70	0	5	10

B. Now add up the scores for each question as follows:

Question 1 + 8 + 15 + 22 + 29 + 36 + 43 + 50 + 57 + 64 = _____

This gives you a score for elements in your writing life such as planning, coordination, management and your personal vision but also touches on the core vacuums you have developed (or not) to power your story.

C. Add up the totals for the following questions:

Question 2 + 9 + 16 + 23 + 30 + 37 + 44 + 51 + 58 + 65 = _____

This gives you a score for the stage of development of character vacuums and other fundamental elements.

D. Add up these totals:

Question 3 + 10 + 17 + 24 + 31 + 38 + 45 + 52 + 59 + 66 = _____

This gives you a score for the area of reader acquisition and anything to do with attracting attention: namely linear, mystery, moral and core vacuums.

E. Add up these totals:

Question 4 + 11 + 18 + 25 + 32 + 39 + 46 + 53 + 60 + 67 = _____

This gives you a score for anything to do with commitment from readers. How effective are the vacuums in your fiction in grabbing and holding reader attention?

F. Add up these totals:

Question 5 + 12 + 19 + 26 + 33 + 40 + 47 + 54 + 61 + 68 = _____

This gives you a score for anything to do with the actual production of stories themselves, including the delivery of a workable plot. Are the vacuums working together to produce a viable plot which moves the reader forward?

G. Add up these totals:

Question 6 + 13 + 20 + 27 + 34 + 41 + 48 + 55 + 62 + 69 = _____

This gives you a score for anything to do with the quality of the writing, or making it fit the readers' needs exactly at a word and sentence level.

H. Add up these totals:

Question 7 + 14 + 21 + 28 + 35 + 42 + 49 + 56 + 63 + 70 = _____

This gives you a score for anything to do with the overall effect, or making sure that your initial idea actually gets to the reader.

The analysis can now give you a graph of each aspect of your writing and its relation to other aspects.

Look at the following example graph.

Note that the top band of the graph, between 75 and 100, what could be called a 'Summer' position, would be the best position for any writing or any of these aspects of a piece of fiction. Here, everything comes together: ideas are strong, even profound; basics like character vacuums are well-constructed and perhaps even beautiful; emotional commitment occurs relatively easily, but without becoming sentimental. We commit to the story, we even love the story and it seems to fulfil needs in us as readers that we didn't even know we had. These are the great stories, including the re-read classics, the mighty works of prose and drama which are immortal. These are the tales that take us to the heights.

Between 50 and 75 would be the next best position, the 'Spring' position. Here, almost everything comes together: ideas are good, though perhaps not wide-ranging; character vacuums are sufficient to

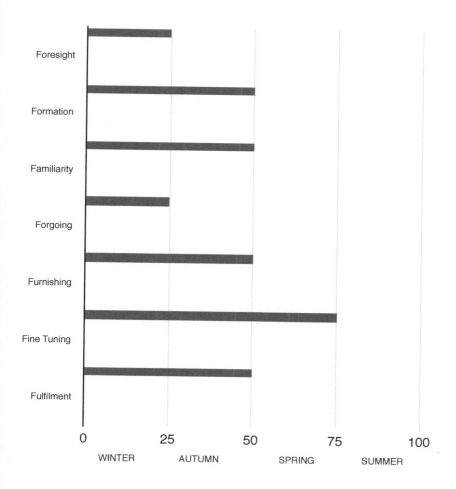

attract our attention to a protagonist; emotional pull exists, but is perhaps over-stated in places. We commit to the story to a degree, and it serves us well. These are the good stories. We may re-read them, we may be very fond of them despite their flaws.

Between 25 and 50 would be a worsening position, or 'Autumn'. Stories start to fail here: ideas are noticeably lacking or slightly awry; character vacuums are weak or non-existent; readers feel detached. Reading these tales feels a bit like a chore - readers resist commitment. Nothing has much impact and it doesn't seem like the writer is that interested in us. The work lacks vacuum power, simply put. We take away little sense of fulfilment, and are critical of the work once we're done.

And obviously between 0 and 25 would be the worst position, 'Winter'. These tales strike us as dire; they lack reality, characters lack any vacuum power and are unattractive not because they are meant to be but because they have been poorly constructed; we reject the story almost entirely, find the plot difficult to engage with or follow and the whole thing is a real effort to get through. Far from serving any needs we may have as readers, these stories seem lost in their own world and communicate little of any significance to us, even if we try very hard. Vacuum power is entirely missing.

Obviously, the thing to aim for is the top part of the graph, 'Summer': something that will last and live in people's hearts.

Firstly, in the example above, look at Column 1: vacuums are weak, perhaps half-formed or unclear even to the writer.

Somehow, in Column 2, the writer has come up with character vacuums that work to a degree, though they lack the power to get into the top half of the graph.

Column 3 shows a similar level of desire - vacuums are attracting some sympathy, but not enough. This is shown in Column 4 - readers, or the writer himself or herself, hasn't committed sufficiently to the piece as a whole. This pale level of emotional investment means that the work is barely surviving - it lacks life and meaning, it lacks vacuums.

Nevertheless, as we can see in Columns 5 and 6, something is happening: the story hangs together (just) and some readers at least feel that their needs are being met as the tale goes along. But Column 6 doesn't get to the top half of the graph.

In summary, it looks like this writer is struggling to produce a reasonable story with a lot of work going on reader wish-fulfilment to keep it running, but the overall work isn't having a powerful enough effect on enough people, perhaps not even on the writer, leaving emotional commitment low.

It's a common kind of X-Ray graph: what it shows is a writer working hard but without knowing any of the fundamentals outlined in this book.

Feeling this to be the case, the majority of writers feel that the remedy is to *insert more into* the story - more scenes, more action, more witty dialogue. The truth is that the story would benefit from *having things taken out of it.*

It lacks vacuums: gaps, needs, emptinesses, desires, missing items, losses, threats.

Stringing a good story together based on what you feel the reader wants to read is easy enough; creating living characters who extract a meaningful emotional commitment from readers and developing a story which satisfies needs that the reader didn't even know he or she had? That's not so easy - not at least until this book.

Another example graph follows.

In this writing, we can see that, while the writer's ideas are still weak (as shown by the first column) and plot vacuums are flagging (as shown by the fourth column), there are relatively stable character vacuums (second column) producing just enough reader commitment to get the reader reading the book which then just about adequately produces a result.

What should this writer concentrate on?

It looks as though there are sufficiently well-developed character vacuums to produce some reader commitment, so boosting linear, mystery, moral and core vacuums, making sure that needs are created and then being met, should push the whole piece up into the top band.

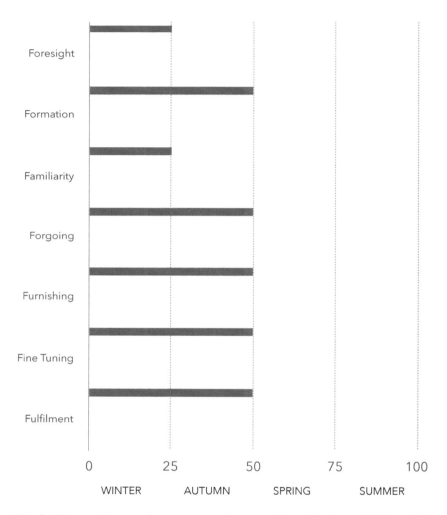

	0	25	50	75	100
	WINTER	AUTUMN	SPRING	SUMMER	

Weak ideas right at the start tend to produce fiction which, while satisfactory, will be cast aside and probably never read again. Think of the 'pot boiler', the mass-produced thriller, the near-copies of great books - these are the works which sustain a reader through a reasonable story using vacuum power, but in the end fail to produce the strong emotional impact or even life-transforming sensation of greater works. Core vacuums are weak, in other words.

Another example follows.

This is a piece of writing in much better shape than any looked at so far.

The graph shows that the writer is reasonably confident that his or her vision is being accomplished (and even that he or she *has* a vision in the first place); that there is almost an abundance of strong, emotionally attractive character vacuums and other vacuums to get the job done.

The area that is letting this particular piece down is *Fulfilment*. There appears to be some difficulty with filling the core vacuum. This is on the edge of being in the lowest position and would need to be addressed as a priority to ensure that the piece does well overall.

How could this happen?

Usually, this results when a writer has slipped up at some point during what is an otherwise well-constructed and emotionally powerful piece. We've all read novels like this: everything is going along fine, we are entertained and make a commitment to the work, and then suddenly there's a mis-step - a character that shouldn't have died at that point is killed; a scene strikes us as being emotionally inappropriate; an important plot point is left hanging. We can, as readers, 'patch this up' in our heads - and this is a significant ability and trait which comes to the fore when we have emotionally invested in a work - but our sense of *fulfilment* suffers: we know, deep down, that the work is flawed.

TV shows are prone to this. We follow episode after episode of our favourite programmes and then there's 'that episode' where 'that' happened - we don't agree, we don't like it, and we find ourselves 'self-editing' the show to some degree to get rid of the offending scene or event or character change or whatever it is. We carry on liking the show, we loyally watch the rest of the episodes - but from that point on

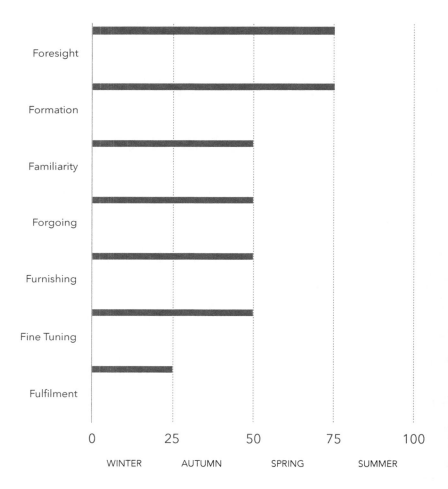

Foresight

Formation

Familiarity

Forgoing

Furnishing

Fine Tuning

Fulfilment

0   25   50   75   100

WINTER   AUTUMN   SPRING   SUMMER

we know that it can never quite reach the top level of fulfilment in our minds.

Of course, as we have mentioned, these diagrams are only a snapshot of the position of any piece of writing, as revealed by the person answering the questions. But the graphs do externalise the views that are in the head of whoever is doing the questionnaire. It becomes instantly and clearly visible where in the writing that person sees the problem as lying.

The graphs show an 'X-ray' of any piece of writing, based on the answers to the questions. You can see through the meat to the bones. Without all the parts of that 'skeleton' in place, at some point your fiction will collapse. More to the point, the lowest column on any one of the graphs is where the most attention is needed.

In the first example, addressing the central ideas of the writer - what does he or she actually want to say? - would generate core vacuums which would turn around the whole thing and consolidate any gains.

In the second example, the core ideas along with the generation of plenty of other vacuums are the points to handle.

In the third example, whatever that slip-up was that lead to a downfall in fulfilment would need to be tackled as a priority.

In your own writing, whatever has shown up as the lowest column is the hottest section to handle: address it fully and the whole operation will be transformed and secured. This gives us our first piece of key advice, which will arise again and again in different forms as you proceed:

Where there is the greatest sense of something missing, there also is the greatest potential.

The trick is to spot what is most missing. The X-Ray Analysis helps you to do that.

Combining the different questionnaire results from others - if you're willing to ask them about your work! - will help you to isolate this further. Some results may be different to yours; some may uncannily reflect your own answers. Either way, the analysis is a useful tool for improving your fiction with the greatest efficiency. You don't have to worry about wasting time focusing on something that might not matter - the X-ray has pinpointed the main issues. Get to work on them and your writing will move out of the dangerous levels and into a better position.

What You Should Do Now

So once you have put your writing through the analysis above, what's next?

• Go through the analysis again and fill in any blanks or points where you couldn't think of anything the first time.

• List out your potential readerships based on what you have now glimpsed.

• Ask yourself what are the main points of change that you now want to make in your fiction based on what you have gleaned here.

• Get the companion volume *How Stories Really Work - A Practical Manual to Transform Your Fiction.*

• Write down any questions you might have and visit the Frequently Asked Questions page at www. clarendonhousebooks.com for further advice or help.

• Do the *How to Write Stories That Work - and Get Them Published!* e-course, which will walk you through all these principles and the process of getting a work in print and in your hands! This is available on the website.

This is just the beginning of your adventure. Right now, you've seen through your fiction to its bones, assessed its 'temperature' and general fitness level, and have discovered the prime motivational force behind fiction and how to harness it to produce potentially limitless effects. If you want to know how to set up your life to make your writing dreams come true, visit

www.clarendonhousebooks.com

Happy writing! I look forward to hearing from you!

-Grant P. Hudson

Appendix:
A Glossary of Vacuums

vacuum: *'A space entirely devoid of matter; a space or container from which the air has been completely or partly removed; a gap left by the loss, death, or departure of someone or something formerly playing a significant part in a situation or activity.'*

A vacuum is defined as that emptiness or absence of something which draws anyone or anything in the vicinity of the vacuum towards whatever it is that is missing.

Magnitude of Vacuums

Universal vacuums: minor losses or threats, inconveniences, grievances, grudges - the kinds of things which are widely experienced by readers in ordinary life. Protagonists of various kinds experience these in the initial parts of successful stories.

Common vacuums: more serious losses or threats, missing education, loss of companionship, loss of proximity to family or home, including loss of family or friends, etc.

Basic vacuums: extreme threats, risks to health, well-being, life, loss of the society or the world. Basic vacuums equate with *core vacuums* in an effective story (see below).

Types of Character Vacuums

External positive character vacuums: these could include escape to a better place, a healthier world-view, a better relationship with someone and so on - things external to the character.

Internal positive character vacuums: these include things like a peace of mind a character would like to achieve, a state of fitness they want to reach, an emotion they'd like to express and so forth, part of the character's internal world.

External negative character vacuums: these could be things like declining health, insecurity in the character's environment, a hungry family or a forthcoming redundancy - real, external factors.

Internal negative character vacuums: including the fear of a future health problem, hunger, pain or personal depression or anxiety and so on - mainly psychological aspects.

Types of Plot Vacuums

Linear vacuums: gaps, needs, holes, threats of loss or other missing things which drive the plot (and the reader) forward along the lines of the question 'What will happen next?' Linear vacuums are the basis of almost all stories and are the most frequently used device in story-telling. They help to create *momentum.*

Mystery vacuums: unknowns, puzzles, enigmas, uncertainties, gaps in knowledge which attract reader attention and stick it to the story along the lines of the question 'What is really going on?' Mystery vacuums are most obviously seen in the detective story sub-genre but are also very common in fiction. They create *'glue'.*

Moral vacuums: dilemmas of choice, uncertainties as to the rightness of decisions or action, moral options along the lines of the question 'What is the right thing?' These punctuate successful stories and engage the moral sense of the reader. They help to create *meaning.*

Core vacuums: central, serious, world-threatening, potentially devastating disasters which address the fundamental issues of the story and consist of answers to the question 'What is this story really all about?' These should be basic vacuums (see above) and should form an effective engine for the story. All other vacuums are designed to attract and hold reader attention and drive it towards and into core vacuums.

See also the Table of Vacuums below.

A Table of Vacuums and Genres	COMEDY/ ROMANCE	EPIC	TRAGEDY	IRONY
Character vacuum(s)	are successfully filled through marriage or its equivalent (e.g *Four Weddings and a Funeral, Pride and Prejudice*)	are successfully filled through some kind of transcendent or maturing experience (e.g. *The Lord of the Rings*, the Arthur legends)	are exposed, left unfulfilled and end in death (e.g. *Macbeth, King Lear*)	are exposed, magnified and left unfulfilled (e.g. *Fight Club, An Inspector Calls*)
Linear vacuum(s)	Unexpected sequences of 'What will happen next?' scenarios, answered unexpectedly (resulting in humour)	Expected sequences of 'What will happen next?' scenarios, answered within an expected framework (resulting in drama)	Expected sequences of 'What will happen next?' scenarios, left predictably unanswered (resulting in a sense of loss or pity)	Unexpected sequences of 'What will happen next?' scenarios, left unanswered unexpectedly (resulting in horror or introversion)
Mystery vacuum(s)	Mysteries resolved	Mysteries resolved	Mysteries unresolved	Mysteries unresolved
Moral vacuum(s)	Morality tested but proven	Morality tested but proven	Morality tested but fails	Morality tested but fails
Core vacuum(s)	Risk to wider social fabric resolved	Risk to wider social fabric resolved	Risk to wider social fabric partially resolved	Risk to wider social fabric unresolved

CLARENDON HOUSE PUBLICATIONS
PART OF THE GOLDEN AGE OF INDEPENDENT PUBLISHING

The Clarendon House Library is the home of the 'How to Write Stories That Work -And Get Them Published!' e-course and a huge number of other resources to help you write, publish and market your book, and much more! The idea is to save you time, money and frustration in writing and publishing your own work. You'll find many articles here about writing and creativity, publishing and marketing. You'll also find material to help you run your writing life like a business, and much more!

All the materials are easy to read, informal in style and get swiftly to the point that the reader is most interested in. Many come with charts, diagrams and templates so that the reader can rapidly adapt what is learned and apply it quickly to, for example, a small business, a work of fiction, an essay or a personal relationship.

Clarendon House Publications is a small, independent publisher based online and in the UK. It is for anyone interested in writing (including fiction, essays, copywriting and anything to do with Doctor Who, comics, J. R. R. Tolkien, C. S. Lewis, literature) and much more. Get a free catalogue from the website and find out how you could benefit!

grant@clarendonhousebooks.com

www.clarendonhousebooks.com

Phone: +44 (0)7738 447764

Clarendon House
Publications Packages

Find out how YOU can get published!

Free Fiction Self-Assessment Questionnaire

Do the Fiction Self-Assessment Questionnaire and 'X-Ray' your work
to pinpoint where its strengths and weaknesses lie!

General Advice £45

Get the advice which will point your work in the right direction for
success!

Foundation to Publishing £395

Receive a tailor-made, comprehensive programme of help for your
fiction including
Ideas Workshop
Character Construction
Attracting Readers
Emotional Commitment
Plot Structuring
Quality of Style
Fulfilling Expectations

Basic Publishing Package £1,995

Get published! Package includes
Ideas Workshop
Character Construction
Attracting Readers
Emotional Commitment
Plot Structuring
Quality of Style
Fulfilling Expectations

Full Proofreading & Editing

Preparing for Publication including Correct Formatting, Page Numbering etc

Publication to Your Exact Specifications

Marketing Programme (including options to appear on Amazon, Barnes & Noble, etc)

BONUS ADDITIONAL MATERIAL on How to Succeed in Business as a Writer!

BONUS ADDITIONAL MATERIAL on How to Achieve Your Personal Goals!

Simply visit

www.clarendonhousebooks.com

or email

grant@clarendonhousebooks.com

for details!

Clarendon House
Essay Writing Help

Been given an essay to write?

Staring into space wondering how to begin?

You know your subject - or you thought you did - and you've been given a question to write about that you should be able to tackle. But the blank page or screen is daunting: how will you ever get past it? And then you've been told your essays need to be more 'logical' and your 'argument' needs to be better. What do those things even mean?

Over 20 years' experience in teaching people of various ages how to write essays has provided a few guidelines that have been proven to help students

• get past the blank screen or page and get started
• put together a convincing argument that follows a basic logic
• improve results by at least one whole grade per essay.

Whatever your subject, there are some guidelines that you can use to help you get started and improve your expected grade.

And they are FREE. Simply visit 'Essay Writing Help" at

www.clarendonhousebooks.com

and you'll be able to download the guidelines within seconds.

You'll also be able to get help with a specific essay, all the way through to the final draft. Visit us now!

Clarendon House
Proofreading and Editing

If you need a basic proofreading/editing function done, these are the kinds of things I would look for and fix in your work.

1) Tone or Mood

2) Positioning

3) Logical Flow

4) Grammar

5) Consistency of Style

6) Region-Specific Spelling and Jargon

7) Logical Images

8) Data and Image Attributions

9) Spellcheck

10) Broken Links

Email me at

grant@clarendonhousebooks.com

with an outline of your work and the job you want done. I'll give you an estimate of the number of hours it will take. Proofreading and editing hours cost £45 each, with a minimum order of two hours. (Discounts are available.)

CLARENDON HOUSE PUBLICATIONS
PART OF THE GOLDEN AGE OF INDEPENDENT PUBLISHING

Phone: +44 (0)7738 447764
E-mail: grant@clarendonhousebooks.com

www.clarendonhousebooks.com

Doctor Who

Comics

J. R. R. Tolkien

C. S. Lewis

Literature

Education

Film and Television

and much more!

Visit us now!

How To Write Stories That Work - And Get Them Published! e-course

Your Complete 12 Week Guide to Becoming a Published Author

by Grant P. Hudson B.A. (Hons.)

How to Write Stories That Work - and Get Them Published! e-course

by Grant P. Hudson

This course is very different to anything else on the market. It's not about three act structures, or even particularly about 'writer's journeys' and all the rest of it. It's about the PHYSICS that makes all those other things work in stories.

Everything in this course is based on an extensive 40-year study of English literature and popular fiction, ranging from Shakespeare to contemporary movies like Star Wars or the Marvel superhero films or American television sit-coms. Work examined during the course includes that of master authors like Dickens, Austen, E. M. Forster, C. S. Lewis and many others.

Why are successful works of fiction successful? Their secrets are here!

With this e-course, you're getting a tailor-made, comprehensive programme of help for your fiction, installing successful features of the world's greatest writing PLUS how to get your work actually published AND your published book, with your name on the cover!

Get *How to Write Stories That Really Work - and Get Them Published! e-course* now!

£395.00*

(*Each of the twelve modules is available separately for £45.00 each!)

www.clarendonhousebooks.com

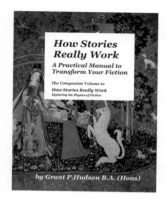

How Stories Really Work - A Practical Manual to Transform Your Fiction

by Grant P. Hudson

This is the companion volume to *How Stories Really Work: Exploring the Physics of Fiction*, which contains explosive new approaches to stories and how to write them. This manual takes you through the key principles of the book step by step, with exercises and practical drills all the way.

Inside, you will find:

• diagrams, tables and graphs to illustrate the ideas set out in the book

• chapter-by-chapter hands-on things to do to build your own piece of working fiction

• exercises to extend and challenge your understanding of your book and of literature and writing fiction.

The product of the Practical Manual is your own work, transformed, with successful components installed that will guarantee more readers and greater satisfaction!

Get *How Stories Really Work - A Practical Manual to Transform Your Fiction* now!

£29.99

www.clarendonhousebooks.com

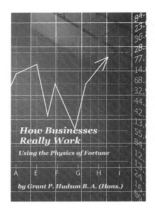

How Businesses Really Work
Using the Physics of Fortune

by Grant P. Hudson

This book could be one of the most powerful weapons you will ever have for transforming your business, your life, and the lives around you. In these pages, you will learn about:

• the *universal patterns* that all businesses follow and how you can use them to boom your business

• the *powerful, hidden force* which motivates customers, employees and your own business, and how to take advantage of it to take your operation to a whole new level

• the business model which, if followed, will create a machine generating *unimaginable numbers of customers and heightened customer satisfaction* for you, based on the most successful businesses in the world.

Along the way, you'll discover:

• the marketing secrets that lie behind super-successful global marketing campaigns like those of Apple or Amazon, and how you can use them in *your* business

• what money really is and how to generate as much as you want, stably and without any kind of 'trick'

• how to tap into the latent power of people and groups around you to support your efforts

and much, much more.

Get *How Businesses Really Work* now!

£19.99

www.clarendonhousebooks.com

How Businesses Really Work
Really Work
A Practical Manual
to Boom Your Business

The Companion Volume to
How Businesses Really Work
Using the Physics of Fortune

by Grant P. Hudson B.A. (Hons)

How Businesses Really Work - A Practical Manual to Boom Your Business

by Grant P. Hudson

This is the companion volume to *How Businesses Really Work: Using the Physics of Fortune*, which contains a revolutionary new look at business and how to make it work for real. This manual takes you through the key principles of the book step by step, with exercises and practical drills all the way.

Inside, you will find:

• diagrams, tables and graphs to illustrate the ideas set out in the book

• chapter-by-chapter hands-on things to do to build your own business

• exercises to extend and challenge your understanding of your business and of marketing, sales, finances, production, quality control and much more.

The product of the Practical Manual is your own business, transformed, with successful components installed that will guarantee more customers and greater revenue!

Get *How Businesses Really Work - A Practical Manual to Boom Your Business* now!

£29.99

www.clarendonhousebooks.com

Also from Clarendon House Publications, by Grant P. Hudson:

How Relationships Really Work
Understanding the Physics of Affinity

Using C. S. Lewis's masterpiece *The Four Loves*, this book asks: Why do some relationships thrive, while others seem doomed?

In this book, you'll also discover the different kinds of love and the parts they all play in your life, what a successful relationship really is and how to base it on truth, and much, much more.

Get *How Relationships Really Work* now!

£19.99

www.clarendonhousebooks.com

How Relationships Really Work - A Practical Manual to Change Your Life

This is the companion volume to *How Relationships Really Work: Understanding the Physics of Affinity*, which contains a new look at love in its many forms and how to construct a successful life. This manual takes you through the key principles of the book step by step, with exercises and practical drills all the way.

Get *How Relationships Really Work - A Practical Manual to Change Your Life* now!

£29.99

www.clarendonhousebooks.com

The London Poems Project Student Workbook

The London Poems Project is a structured course for 11-14 year olds. The course presents a range of approaches to two of the most famous poems ever written, '*Composed Upon Westminster Bridge, September 3rd, 1802*' by William Wordsworth and '*London*' by William Blake examining the poems at the level of theme, style and use of language. It is ideally suited for use in English lessons with whole class groups or with individual children and meets the requirements for Key Stage Three study as outlined by Cambridge University.

Inside this self-contained Student Workbook you will find biographical information on the poets, a comprehensive glossary, line-by-line questions to guide the child through the poems, exercises to extend and challenge the child's understanding of the poems and of literature and writing poetry, and more.

£14.99

www.clarendonhousebooks.com

The London Poems Project Teacher's Guide

Inside this self-contained Teacher's Guide you will find:

•Biographical information on the author

•A comprehensive glossary

•Chapter-by-chapter questions to guide the child through the student workbook

•Exercises to extend and challenge the child's understanding of the book and of literature and writing poems.

•Assessment Guides, Progress Charts, Marking Assistance and a Certificate of Achievement

£14.99

www.clarendonhousebooks.com

The Signalman Project Student Workbook

The Signalman Project is a structured course for 11-14 year olds. The course presents a range of approaches to the famous short story classic by Charles Dickens, *The Signalman*, examining the story at the level of theme, character development and use of language. It is ideally suited for use in English lessons with whole class groups or with individual children and meets the requirements for Key Stage Three study as outlined by Cambridge University.

Inside this self-contained Student Workbook you will find biographical information on the author, a comprehensive glossary, the text of the story and questions to guide the child through the text, exercises to extend and challenge the child's understanding of the text and of literature and writing fiction, and more.

£14.99

www.clarendonhousebooks.com

The Signalman Project Teacher's Guide

Inside this self-contained Teacher's Guide you will find:

•Biographical information on the author

•A comprehensive glossary

•Chapter-by-chapter questions to guide the child through the text

•Exercises to extend and challenge the child's understanding of the text and of literature and writing fiction.

Assessment Guides, Progress Charts, Marking Assistance and a Certificate of Achievement

£14.99

www.clarendonhousebooks.com

The Hobbit Project Student Workbook

The Hobbit Project is a structured course for 11-14 year olds. The course presents a range of approaches to the best-selling children's classic by J.R.R. Tolkien, *The Hobbit*, examining the book at the level of theme, character development and use of language. It is ideally suited for use in English lessons with whole class groups or with individual children and meets the requirements for Key Stage Three study as outlined by Cambridge University.

Inside this self-contained Student Workbook you will find biographical information on the author, a comprehensive glossary, chapter-by-chapter questions to guide the child through the book, exercises to extend and challenge the child's understanding of the book and of literature and writing fiction, and more.

£14.99

www.clarendonhousebooks.com

The Hobbit Project Teacher's Guide

Inside this self-contained Teacher's Guide you will find:

•Biographical information on the author

•A comprehensive glossary

•Chapter-by-chapter questions to guide the child through the book

•Exercises to extend and challenge the child's understanding of the book and of literature and writing fiction.

•Assessment Guides, Progress Charts, Marking Assistance and a Certificate of Achievement

£14.99

www.clarendonhousebooks.com

and much more!

Visit the website today and download your FREE catalogue!

www.clarendonhousebooks.com

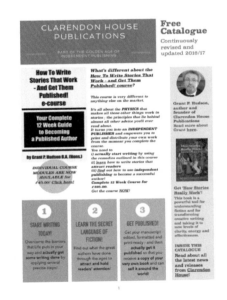

L - #0359 - 140420 - C0 - 210/148/15 - PB - DID2812534